# LEAFING THROUGH MY FAMILY TREE

By

**Jerry R. Davis**

ISBN: 1-933582-26-X
9781933582269

Credits
Cover Artist: Jinger Heaston


Printed in the United States of America

# DEDICATION

**I would like to dedicate this book to my mother and father, Ernestine (Williamson) Davis and Dayton W. Davis.**

Ernestine Williamson &
Dayton Davis
(1929)

# ACKNOWLEDGEMENTS

I wish to thank all the people who made this book a reality. Sabra Steinsiek, Ron Baldwin and Kate Harrington spent many hours proofreading the manuscript. Special thanks should go to Dale Shelby for suggesting the title. I'm very grateful to my mother, Ernestine Davis, who did much of the initial research on which the various stories are based. My cousins, Shirley Tubbs, Glenn Seney, Marjorie Squire, Marian Kosha, Nancy Stine and my brother, Laurel Davis, all contributed to the manuscript. Most of all, I wish to thank my ancestors for being such interesting people and thus making the book possible.

# CONTENTS

**THE DAVIS, JOHNSON & ROSENCRANTS**

**FAMILIES**

(My father's side of the family)

# CHAPTER 1

## RELATIVE STRANGERS

When I think of all the people on this planet to whom I <u>might</u> be related, it simply boggles my mind. Those "relatives who are strangers" surely number at the very least in the thousands, and possibly in the tens of thousands—or even more. When I do the math it is easy to see just how quickly the numbers add up. My father had seven siblings and my mother had ten. Those aunts and uncles produced a total of 24 first cousins for me. The cousins, in turn, had sixty-four offspring. Most of those offspring became parents, grandparents and some are even great grandparents at this point in time. A person's family tree quickly becomes dense with branches and foliage as he or she delves further and further into the family genealogy. It is certainly true that in all likelihood the largest part of our family members are total strangers to us and probably will remain so for the rest of our lives.

Each generation seems to produce a few family members who are interested in doing research and who make the attempt to learn more about the multitude of relatives who are strangers. Of course, in the process they also increase the numbers of their known relatives. I find it amusing and enlightening to see the differences in interest in family history among various members of my own family. My sister, for example, describes genealogy as "about as interesting as watching grass grow." My mother, on the other hand, found it fascinating enough that she spent thousands of hours over a period of about ten years doing family research. When she finished gathering all the information she could on her side of the family, then she turned to my dad's side of the family and did the same with it. I inherited the gene from Mother which prompts me to show an interest in the family and consequently to delve into its history.

Because computer on-line family research had not as yet come into its own at the time when Mother was working on it, she gained most of her information through letters and telephone calls. I remember observing her writing hundreds of letters and carrying on an active correspondence with people as far away from her Michigan home as the states of Vermont, New York, Florida, Washington and California. The connections she made steered her to additional members of the family and those new contacts further enlarged her acquaintance among members of the wide-spread clan.

Though he didn't do the active research or write the letters himself, my father supported Mother's efforts and encouraged her along the way. Dad had a retentive sort of mind filled to overflowing with trivia-type facts about his own family history and the wide variety of relationships contained therein. After I retired I also became interested in our genealogy and, over and over again I was astounded at his almost encyclopedic knowledge of the subject. In one instance I was doing some research on one of my paternal great great grandmothers, Jane (Rosencrants) Stephens. I asked Dad about her and amazingly, without the help of any notes, he listed the names, in order, of the four generations of relatives leading back to Jane. When I checked his listing on the internet, I learned that he had recited the lineage perfectly! Today, after doing years of research on the subject, I still am forced to refer to the family tree in order to emulate his feat.

Not only did my parents get to know their relations through correspondence and telephone calls, but, whenever possible, they also visited them in order to learn to know them on a personal level. After Mother discovered the name of the village in New York State where Dad's ancestors were born and raised, the two of them took one of their driving trips to see it for themselves. Through her research Mother learned that Dad's great grandparents, Ebenezer and Phebe Davis, in 1835 had come to Tuscola County, Michigan from a rural town named Westerlo in Albany County, New York. (See the chapter entitled, "The <u>Actual</u> First Tuscola County Settler.") On that trip Mother and Dad found the little hamlet nestled in the rolling foothills of the Blackhead Mountains a few miles west of the Hudson River.

In Westerlo they made inquires of the natives and, to their surprise, discovered that literally hundreds of Davis descendants still lived in the vicinity. One of the relatives they contacted told them of a lady named Margaret Bogardus, whose husband had been a member of the clan. Margaret, over the past few years, had done a great deal of research on the Davis genealogy. Mother and Dad called on her and she invited them to stay a few days as her guests while the three compared notes on the family. During that first visit Margaret introduced them to a

4

number of the Davises and took them to several of the old family homesteads. In addition, they visited the Westerlo Cemetery where some of the Davis antecedents and other relatives are interred. By combining Margaret's research and hers, Mother was able to broaden immeasurably the scope of her knowledge of the Davis lineage.

On that same New York State trip Mother and Dad first learned of the annual Albany County Area Davis Reunion. Unfortunately they had already missed the get-together for that particular summer but kept it in mind for a future visit to the Westerlo area. The very next year Mother, Dad, my younger brother, Dan, and I all attended the function which was held in a large park along the Hudson River near the city of Albany. There were over a hundred members of the Davis Clan at the get-together and all of them seemed pleased to learn that a small segment of Michigan Davises was in attendance as well.

Through subsequent visits to Margaret's home in Westerlo over the next few years Mother and Dad came to know her and the other New York Davis descendants well. Conversely some of those Davises in that same time period also managed to find their way to Michigan to meet members of the Midwest contingent of the family. The two factions of the large clan were finally reunited after a hiatus extending for nearly a hundred and fifty years.

An additional example of Mother's genealogical research leading to a meeting between disparate segments of our family occurred about that same time, when she and Dad visited her relations in western New York State. That story begins with Mother's maternal grandfather, Carmel Dewain Townsend, being born on a farm near the town of Akron. The tiny village was situated twenty-five miles northeast of Buffalo in a rural part of the state. When he was about thirty years of age, Carmel joined the army. He took part in the Civil War and, after his discharge, abandoned New York State and sought to make his fortune on a small farm in Tuscola County near Vassar, Michigan. Eventually he met and married Sarah Jane Shook who was destined to become my mother's grandmother. (See the chapter entitled, "Ill-fated Sarah Jane Shook.")

Contact between the Michigan Townsends and the New York Townsends ceased to exist after Carmel's death in 1883. That state of affairs continued until the mid 1980s when Mother learned of the existence of two ladies who, like herself, were descendants of Carmel's parents, Asiel and Ruth Townsend. The ladies were Gertrude and

Lucia Churchill and their ancestor was Carmel's elder sister, Lucia. As an interesting side note, they were also related to Winston Churchill, England's wartime Prime Minister. Mother contacted the ladies by letter. The Churchill sisters, who were probably in their mid-eighties at the time, still lived on their family farm near Akron. Neither Gertrude nor Lucia had ever married and both were retired school teachers. The ladies responded to Mother's initial contact with enthusiasm.

Over the next couple of years, Mother and the Churchill women carried on an active correspondence during which they exchanged photos and information with one another about their mutual ancestors. I still have a packet of old family photographs that Lucia and Gertrude sent to Mother at that time. They were eager to see if she could identify the unknown people depicted. Sadly, Mother was unable to do so, but years later my cousin, Nancy Stein, by carefully comparing them with other identified photos, was able to. Through Nancy's efforts we learned that the packet contains pictures of our great great grandparents, Asiel and Ruth Townsend, and several of their thirteen children; plus it included many of their descendants as well.

In the correspondence between the two parts of the family, the Churchills extended an invitation for Mother and Dad to visit them on one of their driving trips east. The invitation was gratefully accepted. Then, since I had recently begun delving into the family genealogy too, my parents asked me to accompany them. I was equally as eager as Mother and Dad to meet and talk to any and all relatives in order to compare notes with them.

We arrived at the Churchill home early in July of 1986 after a six hour drive from Michigan. The Townsend Family residence was a white-painted wood-frame Italianate style house of the Victorian Era. It sat facing the street alongside a short driveway and was the predominant structure in a neat farmstead which also contained a large red barn and several other outbuildings. Gertrude and Lucia greeted us at the door and, for the first time in over a hundred years, descendants of the two branches of the Townsend family actually spoke together face to face.

The Churchills, who had done less than Mother in the way of family research, inundated us with questions about what we had learned about the family. They were equally as curious about our Michigan branch of the clan so we found plenty to discuss during the time we were together. I can remember very few details of the conversations that took place that afternoon, however, I do distinctly recall that we all came away from the visit enthused and gratified about the re-established family contacts.

In this chapter I have included only two of the examples of Mother's research leading to our getting to know various relatives. That does not mean those were the only ones which occurred—far from it. There were many others of a like nature and too numerous to be mentioned in this limited treatment. Through her indefatigable and concentrated research, Mother did more than her fair share of turning "relative strangers" into well-known relatives.

# FAMILY TREE OF JERRY R. DAVIS

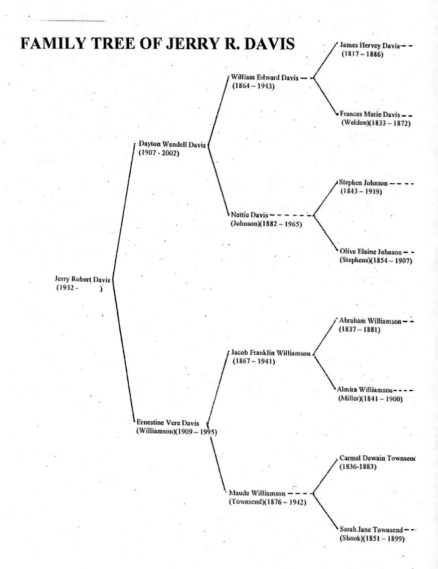

James Hervey Davis
(1817 – 1886)

William Edward Davis
(1864 – 1943)

Frances Marie Davis
(Weldon)(1833 – 1872)

Dayton Wendell Davis
(1907 - 2002)

Stephen Johnson
(1843 – 1919)

Nettie Davis
(Johnson)(1882 – 1965)

Olive Elaine Johnson
(Stephens)(1854 – 1907)

Jerry Robert Davis
(1932 -        )

Abraham Williamson
(1837 – 1881)

Jacob Franklin Williamson
(1867 – 1941)

Almira Williamson
(Miller)(1841 – 1900)

Ernestine Vere Davis
(Williamson)(1909 – 1995)

Carmel Dewain Townsend
(1836-1883)

Maude Williamson
(Townsend)(1876 – 1942)

Sarah Jane Townsend
(Shook)(1851 – 1899)

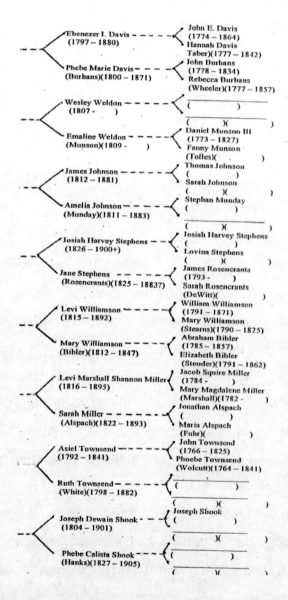

Ebenezer I. Davis
(1797 – 1880)

John E. Davis
(1774 – 1864)
Hannah Davis
Taber)(1777 – 1842)

Phebe Marie Davis
(Burhans)(1800 – 1871)

John Burhans
(1778 – 1834)
Rebecca Burhans
(Wheeler)(1777 – 1857)

Wesley Weldon
(1807 -     )

(                )

(          )(              )

Emaline Weldon
(Munson)(1809 -     )

Daniel Munson III
(1773 – 1827)
Fanny Munson
(Tolles)(          )

James Johnson
(1812 – 1881)

Thomas Johnson
(          )
Sarah Johnson
(          )(          )

Amelia Johnson
(Munday)(1811 – 1883)

Stephan Munday
(          )

(          )(          )

Josiah Harvey Stephens
(1826 – 1900+)

Josiah Harvey Stephens
(          )
Lovina Stephens
(          )(          )

Jane Stephens
(Rosencrants)(1825 – 1883?)

James Rosencrants
(1793 -     )
Sarah Rosencrants
(DeWitt)(          )

Levi Williamson
(1815 – 1892)

William Williamson
(1791 – 1871)
Mary Williamson
(Stearns)(1790 – 1825)

Mary Williamson
(Bibler)(1812 – 1847)

Abraham Bibler
(1785 – 1857)
Elizabeth Bibler
(Stouder)(1791 – 1862)

Levi Marshall Shannon Miller
(1816 – 1895)

Jacob Squire Miller
(1784 -     )
Mary Magdalene Miller
(Marshall)(1782 -     )

Sarah Miller
(Alspach)(1822 – 1893)

Jonathan Alspach
(          )
Maria Alspach
(Fuhr)(          )

Asiel Townsend
(1792 – 1841)

John Townsend
(1766 – 1825)
Phoebe Townsend
(Wolcutt)(1764 – 1841)

Ruth Townsend
(White)(1798 – 1882)

(          )

(          )(          )

Joseph Dewain Shook
(1804 – 1901)

Joseph Shook
(          )

(          )(          )

Phebe Calista Shook
(Hanks)(1827 – 1905)

(          )

(          )(          )

# THE TOWNSEND, SHOOK & WILLIAMSON FAMILIES

## CHAPTER 2

## THE GLASS NEGATIVES

What was the "cutting edge" of photography technology at the beginning of the Twentieth Century? I'm not at all certain that I have the definitive answer to that question but perhaps do have at least a partial one. My maternal grandfather, Jacob Franklin Williamson (always known as Frank), became interested in the new field of photography at a young age. Later Grandfather dabbled in it a bit when he was a young man attempting to earn a living for himself and his new family in Findlay, Ohio. When the Williamsons moved to Vassar, Michigan, at about the turn of the century, he continued that interest while he practiced a variety of different professions.

Eventually Grandfather Williamson found the financial means to purchase a small photography business in Vassar from an elderly man who wished to retire from it. The shop was located on the second floor of a building in the town's center. It was at the northeast corner of the intersection of Main Street and Huron Avenue above a drugstore. Grandfather hired his eldest daughter, Mamie, to work with him as she had recently become a widow. During the couple of years that they ran the shop, Mamie and her young son, Richard, lived in one of its back rooms. Grandpa Frank and Aunt Mamie operated the photography shop for a few years but never were able to make it a real financial success. I find that very surprising because in my estimation he was a high caliber and talented photographic artist.

To produce his photographs, Frank chose the process called *dry plate photography* which involved using glass negatives coated with a light-sensitive gelatin. The thin gelatin layer on the surface of the glass contained the photographic subject's image in reverse. Later, prints could then be made on photo-type paper from the glass negatives. Though the pictures resulting from that process have only black and white images, they are extremely detailed and very clear. Nearly a hundred years after they were filmed, the negatives still produce magnificent pictures. Visual proof of that statement may be found in the fact that many of the photos in this book were developed from them.

The story of how I came into possession of some of Grandfather's glass negatives is a somewhat convoluted one. After a few years of business operation, Frank gave up the photography shop because of failing eyesight and began making fine furniture. He disbanded the photo business but kept some of the negatives along with a part of his photographic collection. The negatives remained in the family even after Grandfather's death in 1941 and eventually came into the possession of his third eldest daughter, Violette May or "Lettie," as she was known. She and her husband, Sam, placed the negatives into two shoe boxes and stored them in a dark corner of their carriage house. Over the ensuing years, everyone in the family, including Lettie, eventually forgot about the negatives and they remained hidden in their safe haven for decades.

When Aunt Lettie died in 1985—a few years after her husband—their home was sold out of the family. In the clean-up process prior to that sale, the boxes of glass negatives were discovered in their secluded corner of the carriage house. No one in the family had any use for or interest in them at the time, so the negatives were shunted to yet another storage place—in the basement of my Cousin Gene Seney's home on Wilmot Street in Vassar. Fortunately, family members had the necessary insight and vision not to destroy them at the time so the negatives remained in another dark corner for nearly a decade longer.

In the early 1990s I began to take an interest in the family genealogy, and as my first project, attempted to assemble as many photographs of my direct ancestors as I could locate. I talked about my quest to anyone and everyone in the family who would listen and earnestly sought their help in finding whatever photos were available. When family gatherings were held, I asked everyone to bring along any old family pictures they could find. One of the relatives with whom I discussed the project was Cousin Gene's wife, Bonnie Seney. Later, when she thought about that conversation, something jogged Bonnie's memory. She recalled Aunt Lettie's death and moving the boxes of negatives from Lettie's carriage house to their basement. Bonnie went looking for the negatives and had no trouble locating them.

The next time I visited the Seneys, Bonnie showed me the boxes and asked if I were interested in having them. Of course I was! I went home and began my investigation by holding each up to a light to see the images it contained. In a short time I realized that I had a family treasure in my possession. In all there were sixty-two glass negatives plus 123 film negatives of the type we are familiar with today. Various members of the family and their friends make up most of the subject matter in both sets of negatives, so I was able to identify them easily. Because a part of his photography business involved taking shots of local points of interest and then making them into picture post cards, there also are some scenic views of Vassar and its environs. In addition I noted a few depictions of larger cities which probably were taken when Grandfather Williamson traveled around the state.

In the dozen-plus years since they have been in my possession, I have examined each of the glass negatives carefully and have had many of them developed into photographs. Understandably, because of the lengthy time involved, a few of them came to me damaged. Usually the gelatin image had managed to separate from the glass surface and became torn in the process. However, I'm pleased to report that the majority of the negatives are still intact and consequently now form the nucleus for a valuable treasure trove of Williamson family photographs. Today's members of the clan owe Grandfather Frank a real debt of gratitude for the negatives.

# CHAPTER 3

## DRAWING MY FAMILY HISTORY

Several years had elapsed after I retired from teaching before I began following in my mother's footsteps by studying our family's history. My research was a bit different from hers in that I particularly wanted to collect pictures of my direct ancestors. One of the first of those I was able to locate was a drawing of my maternal great great grandfather, Levi Williamson. The drawing had appeared, along with a short biography, in a book about noteworthy residents of Michigan's Huron County in the late 1800s. Levi emigrated to the state from Ohio in 1863 and not only was he a farmer who homesteaded near Gagetown, but he was a medical doctor as well.

Great great grandfather Levi's homestead, which I later learned was named Spring Hill Farm, remained as Williamson property for over a hundred years until 1983. At that time his last granddaughter passed away, and the acreage was bequeathed out of the family. Soon thereafter, the new owner sold the farm to the Michigan State Department of Natural Resources to be used as a wild game preserve. Apparently the department officials were interested in the plot of land mainly because of the many animals including deer, foxes, wild turkeys and others that lived there.

Shortly after the Michigan DNR acquired the farm, the house and all the outbuildings except for the barn were bulldozed to the ground. The barn still stands today, but is the only surviving structure. I had never been on the property when it belonged to the family consequently I had no idea how the original farmstead looked. One day my curiosity got the best of me so I drove the fifty or so miles from my home in Midland, Michigan to the

Gagetown area in order to learn more about that part of my family heritage.

Through research I had learned approximately where the old farmstead had been and I was determined to find it. To do so, I rapped on the front doors of several neighboring houses and asked about the farm. One lady, who lived across from the former driveway to the homestead, informed me that she had once been a hired girl at the Williamson home. She pointed to a remote barn that we could just see through the thicket of trees across the road and told me that was the place. The farm buildings had been situated in the center of the farmstead with two long driveways leading to the neighboring roads on the north and the west. Because the nature preserve was fenced, I was forced to park my car on the edge of the property along Williamson Road about a half mile away. After traipsing through the thicket which at one time had been the north driveway, I located the area where the farm buildings once stood. Williamson Road, by the way, was named after my ancestor, Levi Williamson.

Since it was the only intact building on the site, I examined the gambrel-roofed barn first. During that exploration some interesting thoughts crossed my mind about the possibility of family ghosts continuing to inhabit the structure. Initially I entered the barn's basement which still contained the horse stalls, the cow stanchions and a few box stalls for the younger cattle. Then I made my way to the upper threshing floor in the same manner that the old horse-drawn hay wagons had done it—that is, by following deep wheel ruts in an earthen ramp at the front of the barn. While I stood in the open doorway, the wind made eerie moaning sounds as it whistled through the cracks between the vertical boards forming the sides. Once inside, I climbed a wooden-rung ladder to the hay mow and looked out over what once had been the Williamson fields. As I watched, a startled deer dashed across an open field seeking cover in the heavier woods across the way.

When my curiosity about the barn was satisfied, I turned to what was left of the other buildings on the farmstead. One of those was a sort of garage or carriage house which not only had a storage loft above the main floor, but a cellar below it. The building merely had been bulldozed over toward the north and all the materials were still there in a haphazardly compacted condition. The cellar level clearly had been used as a chicken coop and that part of the structure was still pretty much intact.

At the granary I found the same thing—the bulldozer had merely shoved the building off its foundation and, of course when it was moved, the structure collapsed. The same was true of the privy and the tool shed as well. During my fascinating exploration of the homestead, I even found flower beds, berry bushes plus many ornamental trees and hedges that had been planted by the Williamsons when they had still occupied the farm.

The old farmhouse I left for last, as it was merely an unhappy looking pile of debris. The wreckage which remained gave absolutely no hint of what the house had looked like in its heyday. Even the basement foundation was bulldozed and the remaining cavity had been filled in.

What a shame, I thought, that I had never seen the home before it was destroyed. The only recognizable part that remained was a small section of a stairway with three or four of the steps still intact. However, it was a stairway that led nowhere.

From that first visit to the Williamson homestead the small seed of an idea began to germinate in my mind. In time it developed into a burning desire to learn what Spring Hill Farm's buildings (in particular the house) had looked like when the Williamsons lived there. I have always enjoyed drawing and decided to put that talent to use in preserving the homestead, at least on paper. My first step toward that goal was to visit my mother and dad who had been to the farm many times through the years. Mother, who was already in her mid eighties and very shaky, drew a rough sketch of the outside of the house and then a somewhat basic floor plan of each of the two levels. By that time her memory and drawing skills were failing badly but the unsophisticated, and I found out later, inaccurate, drawings were just the start that I needed.

I went home and got out my drawing board to make the first of what turned out to be many renderings of the house and out buildings. When I finished each drawing I took it to Mother and Dad to get their critical comments. Then I went back to the drawing board to incorporate their suggested changes. Ever so slowly an image of the Williamson family home and farmstead began to take shape once again.

Dad and Mother told me about another relative—a man named Harold Proudfoot—who lived in Sebewaing. They knew that he would be even more familiar with the buildings because he had spent a great deal of time at the farm during the 1970s and 80s. He had managed the financial affairs of the last surviving Williamson granddaughter, Zella Mae (Williamson) Marshall, during the final years prior to her death. Zella Mae had lived in the house all of her ninety-five years.

I visited Harold and his wife, Evelyn, told them of my quest and showed them the drawings. They suggested several changes about the house that they remembered from having been there. They also gave me the address of another relative, Dolores Bauder, in Wisconsin who had a watercolor painting of the farmhouse. I wrote to Dolores and asked if she would send me a photo of the painting. She did that and though it did help me somewhat, its value was limited. The picture only showed the south side of the house which was its narrowest side, whereas my drawings showed the house from all views.

After many trips back and forth between my parent's home and mine, plus others to Harold and Evelyn's home, and further visits to the homestead, I ended up with drawings that show the house, including its floor plans, the garage, the granary, the tool shed and even the privy. In addition, I drew a map of the homestead showing the relative locations of the various buildings, including the old barn. In order to correctly situate the different farm buildings on that map, I paced off the distances between the piles of debris and then made notes which I transferred to the drawings at home.

I'm certain that the renderings aren't exactly correct in all ways but they are close enough to give one a good idea of how the old house and farm buildings appeared when they were owned and inhabited by my Williamson relatives. As an interesting side note, a few years after I finished the drawings of the buildings, I found a couple of photographs of the front of the Williamson home in a slide collection belonging to my mother.

From the first time I visited the Spring Hill Farm site I was saddened to think that it had been so callously destroyed. I thought, "What a real shame it would be if memories of the first Williamson Family farm in Michigan were to die with my mother and her generation of kinsmen." Therefore my research and the resulting drawings were done to preserve some little part of our heritage for present and future members of the family and for posterity.

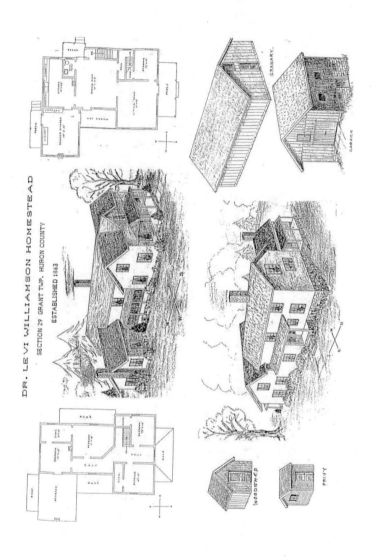

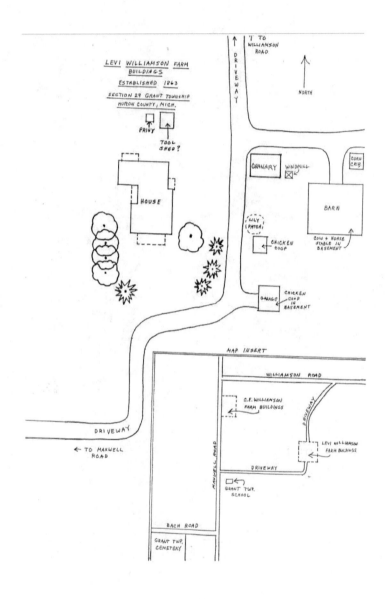

## CHAPTER 4

## THE WILLIAMSONS & SPRING HILL FARM

Great Great Grandfather Levi Williamson homesteaded in Grant Township and in doing so was the first white settler in that area of Huron County, Michigan. According to my mother's writings, Levi visited the unpopulated site a year previous to moving there from Ohio in order to select an acreage which suited his needs. As a medical doctor he used the products of trees and herbs in order to concoct some of his homemade remedies, so he wanted to settle in an area where those grew naturally. Levi's other criteria included the following: the land had to have a natural spring supplying good water and it had to be located in an area high enough to avoid the springtime floods. Also, it must include a woodlot capable of producing the timbers and other lumber for his farm buildings, maple trees to provide syrup and sugar for his family, and it must have rich soil for the crops he planned to grow.

The eighty acre site the doctor chose for his homestead was in section twenty-nine of that township which is situated at the junction of present day Williamson and Maxwell Roads with Tuscola County bordering it on the south. Levi named his acreage "Spring Hill Farm" and the Williamsons lived and worked there for the next 120 years. In 1983 Levi's granddaughter, Zella Mae (Williamson) Marshall, died. In her will she left the farm to a man who lived in Bad Axe. He had promised her that he would keep the acreage intact as a family farm after her death, but soon broke that promise.

Zella Mae Williamson was the daughter of John Williamson, Levi's second son from his second wife, Agnes Cellars. Agnes and Levi had married after his first wife, Mary, died while giving birth to their fifth child. John grew to adulthood on his father's farm and on Christmas Day in 1884, he married Susan Cosgrove, a neighbor girl. John and his new family continued living and working on the farm after his mother, Agnes, inherited it at Levi's death in 1892. Ownership of Spring Hill Farm finally passed to John twenty-one years later when Agnes died in 1913. He was fifty-three at the time.

John and Susan had three children in all. The eldest, Agnes Levina, was born in 1886, Zella Mae was born in 1888 and the youngest, Willamina Victoria, joined the family two years later. The three girls were raised on Spring Hill Farm. Little is known about the youngest, Willamina, other than that she died at a young age. The eldest, Agnes, became a milliner in Ann Arbor, Michigan but succumbed to a diabetic coma in 1912. After completing high school, Zella Mae entered the University of Michigan. She was graduated in 1912 with a master's degree in science and a certificate to teach. She taught for a number of years in various high schools around the Thumb Area of Michigan.

Zella Mae's father died in 1934 when she was forty-six. Both of her sisters had already passed away, so Zella Mae inherited Spring Hill Farm. She returned to her birthplace with the idea of managing it with hired help. Eventually she located Neil Marshall who was willing to work the place. Zella Mae, by that time a typical "old maid school teacher," felt it would be unseemly for Neil to live in the farm home with her because they were not married. According to my mother, that is the reason that they were wed in 1937 when she was 49 and he was 47. Mother hinted also that the marriage was strictly platonic and that Zella Mae, during the seventeen years they were married, always slept in the small downstairs bedroom at the front of the house while Neil slept in one of the upstairs bedrooms at the back.

Regardless of their sleeping arrangements, the relationship and the farm prospered. Neil was a hard-working, intelligent man who treated the land with the utmost respect so it produced well under his guidance and direction. Zella Mae was equally hard-working and intelligent and they made an excellent team.

I was a teenager during much of the Marshalls' marriage and I can recall only one occasion of meeting them. It happened when I was showing my Hereford steer as a 4-H Club exhibit at the week-long Tuscola County Fair in Caro during the mid 1940s. One day Zella Mae and Neil visited the fairgrounds and, if my memory serves me correctly, my older brother, Laurel, recognized the couple and introduced them to me. My impressions were that they were very tall (I was only twelve or thirteen), they exhibited no humor or warmth, in fact they looked grim, and I noted that they both were dressed in plain, almost severe, black clothing. The pair seemed very quiet and extremely reticent. We chatted for only a short time because we obviously had little in common with one another.

The next time I heard anything about Neil and Zella Mae was in 1954 when I was a junior at Michigan State. My mother told me that Neil had been killed in a tragic farm accident. Apparently he was riding on a grain drill (planter) behind his team of horses. A lightening strike spooked the animals and they bolted. Neil fell forward and was run over by the drill. He was killed instantly. The horses halted when they reached the end of the field row, but Neil's dog, ever at his side, ran to the farmhouse where Zella Mae was preparing a meal. She saw the dog and, sensing that something was horribly wrong, rushed to the field to investigate and found her husband's mutilated body.

Unable to run the farm on her own, Zella Mae who was sixty-six at the time, rented the fields of Spring Hill Farm to neighbors and resumed her teaching career. One of her teaching positions after that incident was at the St. Josaphat Catholic Elementary School in Carrollton Township near Saginaw. Here is an interesting item about her time there. She boarded with a family named Bader. The Bader's son, Allen, married a sister-in-law to my older brother and so we still have contact with them. In fact, while researching this story I called the Baders in order to find out what information they had about Zella Mae. They remembered her well and filled me in on a number of details about her life.

In 1964 Zella Mae made application to the Michigan State Historical Commission to have Spring Hill Farm declared a Centennial Farm. That designation meant that the same family had owned the acreage for at least one hundred years. Her Grandfather Levi had homesteaded the farm in 1863. The Historical Commission granted the designation and Zella Mae received a Centennial Farm sign which was placed in the front yard of the farm house.

I'm uncertain when Zella Mae retired from teaching for the second time but eventually she did so and returned to the farm to live out the last years of her life. Long after she died I had the opportunity to read one of the volumes of her diary. It was for the year 1973 and she was eighty-five at the time. I found it extremely interesting that she noted the high and low temperatures each day and indicated what the general weather conditions were. She even wrote down the price of grain, beans, corn and other crops which she heard quoted over the radio. In the diary, Zella Mae commented on the politics of the day and talked about exchanging letters with various relatives, including my mother. During her last years my parents visited her regularly to help with some of the household tasks. My older brother, Laurel, also stayed with her one weekend during that year. Those events all were duly recorded in Zella Mae's diary along with detailed commentary about their visits, what was talked about, what tasks were accomplished and even those chores that were planned but not accomplished. At that advanced age, she still remained a "no nonsense" type of lady.

Laurel wrote to me recently after reading my rough draft of this story. He included an additional memory that he had about a visit to Zella Mae's home.

*"One cold winter night when I was traveling from our folks' place in Gladwin, Michigan to my home in Washington State, I stopped in to visit, and she invited me to stay there over night. She told me that I could sleep in one of the upstairs unheated bedrooms, but that I would need a heated brick for my feet.*

*When it was time for bed, she gave me a warm brick wrapped in a blanket. My feet stayed nicely warm all night, and I had been gently taken back to an era of time which had all but ended prior to my birth. I was thrilled!"*

In October of 1983, when Zella Mae was still living alone at Spring Hill Farm, she fell from the back porch to the sidewalk below. She was badly injured but did manage to drag herself up onto the porch and inside the house where she collapsed on a couch in the dining room. She remained there for several hours until a neighbor, who regularly brought the mail, found her. An ambulance was called and she was taken to the emergency room. After a short hospital stay, she was transferred to a convalescent home but never recovered. On November 4, 1983, Zella Mae, who was ninety-five at the time, died at the group home without ever again setting foot at Spring Hill Farm. As I previously noted, with her death, ownership of the farm passed from the family.

Dr. Levi Williamson
(1815 - 1892)

John M. Williamson
(1854 – 1934)

Zella Mae (Williamson) Marshall
(1888 – 1983)

Neil Marshall
(1890 – 1954)
& his Native American collection

Farmhouse
Spring Hill Farm

# CHAPTER 5

## THE FAMILY FEUD

Probably the most well-known feud in United States history was the one between two families—the Hatfields and the McCoys—in rural Kentucky. A few years ago, when I first began to research my mother's ancestry, unwittingly I came across information which indicated that there was strife between two different segments of the Williamson Family as well. I soon realized that though it never became violent or famous like the Kentucky feud, it was in fact a full-fledged family vendetta lasting for several generations. I learned of the feud through contacts with a distant cousin, Dolores Bauder from Wisconsin, while I was attempting to garner additional information about our common ancestors. Dolores mentioned the severely strained relations in the family in her reply to one of my letters of inquiry.

Dolores related that during the years she was growing up, her family lived in Midland, Michigan, but they occasionally traveled the forty miles to Gagetown, in the Thumb Area of the state, to visit her grandparents. They were Charles E. and Christina (Thompson) Williamson. The grandparents owned a farm on the southeast corner at the intersection of Williamson and Maxwell Roads. Their acreage along Williamson Road was just west of Spring Hill Farm, the original Williamson Family homestead. Spring Hill Farm had access to Williamson Road via a curving driveway to the north and it was connected to Maxwell Road by a long driveway, abutting Dolores's grandparents' farm on the south. (See map of the farms.)

As a child, Dolores was severely warned against playing near the driveway to Spring Hill Farm. According to her family there was "a mean old lady" who lived at the end of the driveway in the woods. Dolores and her siblings were never told that the "mean old lady," who actually was a distant cousin of theirs named Zella Mae (Williamson) Marshall, was related in any way to her family. Dolores's parents and grandparents refused to discuss anything about that part of the family and consequently she and her siblings were completely ignorant of its very existence while they were growing up.

When my mother passed away in 1995, I received all the voluminous papers that were the result of the large amount of family research she had done during the last years of her life. In reading those papers I discovered that Mother also had discussed the feud with our cousin. Mother and Dolores exchanged letters and family information during 1988 and here is an excerpt from one of Dolores's letters dated April first of that year.

*"I do have a question for you, though. I was not aware of any other Williamson family (Mae Williamson Marshall in particular) until a few years ago. Since then I have discovered there had been some kind of a family feud, or something. Do you know what it could have been?*

*Was my grandfather, Charles, on the outs with the rest of
the clan?"*

I don't have a copy of Mother's letter in reply but can
surmise some of what she wrote by reading Dolores's next
letter to her which was dated October 17, 1988.

*"Thank you for sharing your information with me. I
was especially interested in the account that my father
gave you of the Williamson family feud. I guess you can
tell that my immediate family never talked about such
things—even when I asked questions, I never got a
straight answer—almost as if there was something to be
ashamed of—or perhaps it was just taboo to talk about it
in the family!*

*What a shame that so many of us missed out on so
much of our rich heritage because a couple of our
ancestors could not get along together! I don't suppose
we will ever know the real truth—maybe William "Bill"
was upset because his half-brother John ended up with the
farm and as Levi's executor—who knows?"*

Dolores's speculation in the second of her letters brings up the subject of what caused the rift between the Williamsons. Her letter hints at one of the possible causes. When the family patriarch, Dr .Levi Williamson, died in 1892 he had only two living sons. The elder of the two was William who was fifty-two years old. He was the child of Levi's first wife, Mary (Bibler) Williamson. The other was William's half-brother, John, who was thirty-eight and the son of Levi's second wife, Agnes (Cellars) Williamson.

William had already purchased acreage adjacent to Spring Hill Farm toward the west. He and his family lived there and worked that plot of land. John and his family, however, were living on and managing the original Williamson homestead (Spring Hill Farm). John was appointed as the executor of Levi's estate and I assume that the farm was inherited by Levi's widow, Agnes (Cellars) Williamson. When she died twenty-one years later in 1913, the farm passed to her only living son, John. Though that was a logical sequence of events, the net result would be that William and his heirs were, in effect, cut out of their Williamson inheritance. Inheritance problems often cause family rifts, and that could easily have been one of those cases.

Harold Proudfoot, another cousin to the Williamsons, who spent much time at Spring Hill Farm in the 1980s claimed that in addition to the inheritance problem there was another issue which caused the Williamson feud. He surmised that the dispute probably centered on the driveway along the south property line of the William Williamson farm. That driveway allowed access to Spring Hill Farm from Maxwell Road. (See map of the two farms) Harold had been told that the family feud arose over negotiations concerning ownership of that driveway. If that is true, then the John Williamson faction (the Spring Hill Farm group) won out because the driveway remained a part of that farm until well after it was no longer owned by the Williamsons.

Regardless of what caused the dispute, the Williamson Family feud was a fact of life for several generations of the family. It remains today only as a bad memory because all the participants have long since gone to their graves. The present-day Williamsons and their descendants can only surmise about the causes of the family schism. Today neither farm is owned or occupied by anyone connected to the Williamsons. Spring Hill Farm, as previously mentioned, is now a nature preserve owned by the Michigan Department of Natural Resources and the William Williamson acreage is still operated as a farm but under new private ownership. The long driveway from Spring Hill Farm remains as one of the few reminders of the family dispute.

A few years ago, while going to visit the defunct homestead, I attempted to follow that route toward the old farm. The driveway was eroded, rut-filled and nearly impassable for an automobile, and at the end of the driveway I came to a sudden halt at a formidable iron gate. On it was a Michigan Department of Natural Resources sign forbidding passage beyond that point.

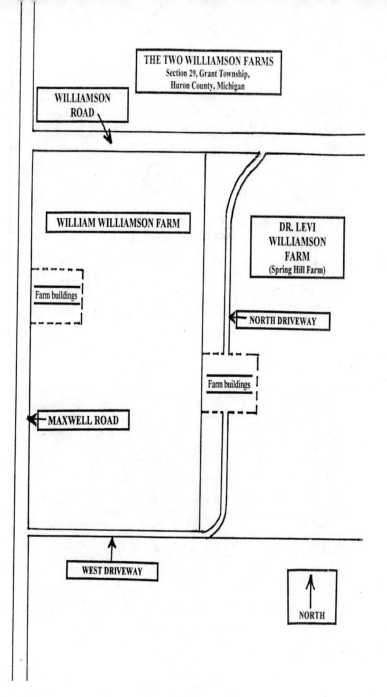

THE TWO WILLIAMSON FARMS
Section 29, Grant Township,
Huron County, Michigan

WILLIAMSON
ROAD

WILLIAM WILLIAMSON FARM

DR. LEVI
WILLIAMSON
FARM
(Spring Hill Farm)

Farm buildings

NORTH DRIVEWAY

Farm buildings

MAXWELL ROAD

WEST DRIVEWAY

NORTH

Farmhouse
Spring Hill Farm
(Destroyed 1983)

Charles Williamson Farmhouse
(2006)

# CHAPTER 6

## A WARRIOR IN THE FAMILY

Throughout history Americans by the millions have served their country during a single international conflict. A few of them have even fought in two wars, but rarely any more than that. One of my great great grandfathers, Joseph Shook, had the distinction of being a part of the United States military during three wars. The first was an Indian border skirmish which technically could not be called a declared war, nonetheless it involved two conflicting armies firing ammunition at one another. The second was the Mexican – American War (1846 – 1848), and the third was the Civil War (1861 – 1865). Most of my information is about Great Great Grandfather Joseph's service in the Civil War but before I get into that part of the story, here is the little I have been able to learn about his background.

Joseph Dewain Shook probably was born in Northumberland County, Pennsylvania in 1804. He lived for a time in Lockport, Niagara County, New York and then in Dover, Cuyohoga County, Ohio when he married Phebe Calista Hanks. The forty-one year old groom and his eighteen year old bride were wed on April 21, 1845. On her marriage certificate, Phebe listed her birth date as June 21,1827, and her birthplace as Rutland, Vermont. Though it has never been authenticated, family lore claims that Phebe Hanks and Abraham Lincoln's mother, Nancy Hanks, were related to one another. Phebe's mother's name was Lucy Hanks but, other than that bit of information and her place of birth, little is known for certain about her family background. That speculation, whether true or false, nonetheless adds interest to Phebe's birth.

According to what is known about where their children were born, Joseph and Phebe, after their marriage, seem to have continued his previous nomadic type of existence. Their eldest son Lewis's birth place was Cuyohoga County near Akron, Ohio in 1846. Where their second and third children, Harvey, and Sarah Jane, were born is not known. However, their fourth child, Elsie Ann, was born in 1854 in Vermillion on the Lake Erie coast of Ohio. Yet by 1861, when Joseph enlisted to fight in the Civil War, the family apparently had moved to the vicinity of Fort Wayne, Indiana because his military record lists that as his place of enlistment. He joined Company C of the Forty-fourth Regiment of the Indiana Volunteers but for some inexplicable reason, at his discharge, was mustered out of Company D (instead of Company C) a little less than two years later. (My guess would be that the original Company C was decimated by losses at the Battle of Shiloh and the few remaining soldiers were then transferred to Company D, but that is pure conjecture.)

The story of Joseph's joining the army to serve in the Civil War is an unusual one. He was already fifty-six years old when he enlisted and had even passed his fifty-seventh birthday by the time he was actually mustered into Company C in November of 1861. His official military record, however, lists his age as forty-four, therefore Joseph must have shaved over twelve years off his correct age on the application. The story became even more complicated but interesting when, through research, we learned that Phebe and Joseph's eldest son, Lewis, enlisted at the same time his father did. Lewis was only fifteen years old at the time but his records show that he added a year to his correct age on his application in order to be accepted. Therefore, both father and son lied their ages to join the Civil War.

Lewis was less fortunate than his father in the Civil War. He was in and out of several different military hospitals during most of the nearly year and a half that he served in the army. In February, 1862, he entered a hospital in Calhoun, Kentucky. In November of that same year he was sent to another facility in Nashville, Tennessee. He died on January 14, 1863 in a military hospital in New Albany, Indiana at the age of seventeen. (Lewis's military record lists his age at death as eighteen because he had given the incorrect age at the time of his enlistment.) His early demise seems logical when one examines Lewis's medical history. Family lore tells us that as a child he contracted measles and the disease permanently affected his lungs. As a result his system was unable to tolerate the primitive conditions that soldiers had to undergo during the war. Lewis's military record indicates that he died of plithisis pulmonulia. I have not been able to verify that as an actual disease, but the "pulmon" part of the second word indicates that it had something to do with the lungs.

Joseph also did not survive the Civil War unscathed. He took part in the fierce fighting at Pittsburg Landing, Tennessee, which is better known as the Battle of Shiloh. It was named for a church located on the battlefield. On the first of the two days of hostilities—Sunday, April 6, 1862—Joseph was wounded in the arm. One of his companions in that battle, John W. Farmer, later wrote the following in an affidavit about Joseph's condition. Mr. Farmer, who hailed from Harlan in Allen County, Indiana, wrote the affidavit in 1889 to assist Joseph in collecting a pension from the federal government for his military service. I found this statement among Joseph's military discharge papers which another relative had requested from the federal government.

*"We [Joseph and Mr. Farmer] were both wounded while engaged in the battle of Shiloh on Sunday, April 6th in 1862. We were together at the landing [Pittsburg Landing] during the whole night following the first day's battle and were both exposed during the whole of said night—to a cold, drenching rain without blankets or shelter of any kind and from the effects of said exposure, the said Joseph Shook contracted rheumatism and kidney trouble and was sent to hospital for treatment."*

Joseph spent most of the next year in several military hospitals and finally was discharged from the army at Murfreesboro, Tennessee on April 29, 1863. The discharging doctor wrote *"During the last two months said soldier has been unfit for service for 61 days by reason of chronic rheumatism and the effects of old age. . . His disability has resulted from exposure and fatigue incident to [caused by] the service."*

Some family members have claimed that Joseph carried the flag for General Sherman in his famous march to the sea from Atlanta, Georgia. However, that claim is disproved by his military records which show that his discharge from the army occurred more than a year and a half before that event took place. Sherman's march started out from Atlanta on November 15, 1864 and Joseph had been mustered out of the military in April of 1863.

One can only wonder how Phebe, Joseph's wife, fared while he was off fighting for his country. The Indian border skirmish in which he participated occurred before they met and married, so that would have had no effect on her. However, the Mexican-American War began about a year after their wedding and just shortly before the birth of their first son, Lewis. Thus she was left at home with an infant while Joseph was gone. Their second son, Harvey, was born in 1849 about a year after the hostilities with Mexico ended. When he joined the Civil War in November of 1861, Joseph took fifteen year old Lewis with him to the army but he left Phebe with the other four children. At that time they included Harvey (12 years old), Sarah Jane (10 years old), Elsie Ann (7 years old) and Philip (5 years old). Joseph's army pay amounted to only $11.00 per month and I doubt that much of that money ever found its way back home to Phebe and the children. What income she and the family survived on during that time is a family mystery.

Some time after Joseph's discharge from the army, the family moved to Vassar, Michigan and that was their home for the rest of their lives. We know that they already lived there in 1873 when their daughter, Sarah Jane who was my great grandmother, met and married my great grandfather, Carmel Townsend. From what I have been able to ascertain, Joseph and Phebe's last five children, Mary, Johnny, George, Charles and Artemis were all born in Vassar. Three of the boys were said to have died of diphtheria, but we don't know exactly when that occurred. Several epidemics of diphtheria swept across the Midwest during the 1870s and 1880s.

The Shook Family's move to Michigan apparently did not help their financial situation. Joseph first applied for an army pension on February 6, 1874. It was refused. He re-applied in 1882 and that second application also was refused. Then in 1889 he applied for a third time with the same result. His next application was denied in 1890. Finally he was granted a small military pension in 1895. It had taken him more than twenty years from the date he first applied to receive a pension of only twelve dollars per quarter. That would figure out to be only forty-eight dollars for the entire year! Of necessity, Joseph held part time jobs until he was ninety-one years of age. He died shortly after the turn of the century in 1901 when he was ninety-seven years of age.

After Joseph's death, Phebe who was seventy-four at the time, applied for a military widow's pension. In order for her to receive the money, she had to prove two things: first that she and Joseph were in fact husband and wife and second, that she was virtually destitute. She had to sign an affidavit that she had been completely dependent on Joseph and that her income at the time was less than two hundred and fifty dollars per year. All of that was for a pension which amounted to a total of eight dollars each quarter—only thirty-two dollars per year! Phebe outlived Joseph by a mere four years and today she lies next to him in a grave under a small stone that has no markings.

Joseph and Phebe Shook's final resting place is in the circle of veterans' graves that surrounds the tall Civil War Monument in the Riverside Cemetery about a mile south of Vassar. Probably the reason Phebe's grave has no markings is that she rests in the area reserved for veterans. To commemorate Joseph's service in three United States' armed conflicts (the Indian border skirmish, the Mexican – American War and the Civil War), a Mrs. K. R. Hill, of Vassar, wrote the following poem in his memory. As a result of her poem, Mrs. Hill's name was entered in Who's Who in America.

## THE DEAD HERO

They laid the old hero down to rest
And the world enthused at his story.
Repeating it o'er with reverent zest
'Til it covered his name with glory.

Thrice had he gone at his country's call
To the field of strife's stern dangers,
To "chance in fight" but not to fail
When peril and death were no strangers.

But to bear from Shiloh's stoned field
The scars of a soldier heroic,
Was a pride that his soul would never yield,
With the listless calm of a stoic.

They laid him tenderly down to rest
And Justice, her white robes upon her
Said, "Wreathe in starry folds on his breast
The flag that he so loved to honor."

He will stand no more in fiery glow
Where the leaden hailstones rattle.
Nay, the brave old soldier of long ago
Has faced and fought his last battle.

Buoyed up by his childlike sweet belief,
Life's merciless storms has weathered.
Now full of years like a golden sheaf
Has been to the Harvest Home gathered.

And, I think, somewhere in the vast beyond
With the olden smile so pleasant,
That he, like a happy child will respond
To the heavenly roll call, "Present."

—Mrs. K. R. Hill
Vassar, Michigan
August 27, 1901

Joseph Dewain Shook
(1804 – 1901)

Phebe Calista (Hanks) Shook
(1827- 1905)

# CHAPTER 7

## ILL-FATED SARAH JANE SHOOK

I remember watching one of Rodney Dangerfield's comedy vignettes on television where he said, *"If I didn't have bad luck, I wouldn't have any luck at all."* Though she lived nearly a hundred years before Dangerfield did, I feel certain that my great grandmother, Sarah Jane Shook, would have said the same thing about her life.

My maternal grandmother's mother suffered more than her own fair share of tribulations and grief during the short forty-eight years that she lived. Sarah Jane was born in 1851 at her parents' home somewhere in Ohio. (Her parents were married in Cuyohoga County and lived in various locations in that state and Indiana at least until the

Civil War was over with.) She was the third child of Joseph and Phebe Calista (Hanks) Shook. Sarah Jane had two older brothers, Lewis and Harvey, and seven younger siblings including two sisters, Elsie Ann and Mary Alice, and five other brothers who were Philip, Johnny, George, Charles and Artemis. The last four all died in infancy or at a very young age.

Family photographs show Sarah Jane to be a plain girl who grew up to be a plain woman. About 1873, when she was twenty-two years old, she met a Civil War veteran, named Carmel Dewain Townsend who, according to his photographs, was very handsome and had piercing eyes that seemed to bore right through a person. Carmel was fifteen years her senior and for his service in the Civil War, had been awarded a small homestead farm three miles southeast of Vassar.

Carmel's youth was spent growing up on his family's farm near Akron in western New York State and he was the eleventh child (out of thirteen) of Asiel and Ruth (White) Townsend. Asiel was descended from an English nobleman who was a loyal supporter of William the Conqueror. Family lore has it that the New York Townsends were well off financially. Asiel died in 1841 just one year after his youngest child was born, but several of his sons and sons-in-law were available to manage the fertile acreage for the family so the Townsends continued to prosper.

Sarah Jane Shook and Carmel Dewain Townsend were married at Vassar in late 1873 or early 1874. They earned a meager living from Carmel's homestead farm and soon began producing a family. Their first child, Winslow James, was born November 8, 1874. He lived less than six months and died in April of the following year. Their second child was my grandmother, Maude Dette Townsend, who was born on April 20, 1876, almost exactly a year after her older brother passed away. Three years later, on August 19, 1879, another daughter, Mabel Augusta, was born. The family was completed when a son, Joseph Dewain, was born on July 5, 1883. However, a dark cloud loomed menacingly on the family's horizon.

Carmel's mother, Ruth Townsend, died on May 10, 1882. Carmel fully expected to inherit a portion of his mother's estate, but was to be sadly disappointed. Ruth Townsend was a bitter and vindictive old woman who felt that most of her children had abandoned her and their home state of New York. At the time of her death, only six of her thirteen children were still alive. Several had died young, others were killed in the Civil War and, of the remaining six, all but three had moved to other states. Ruth punished that perceived lack of loyalty by disinheriting her out-of-state children, including Carmel.

Sarah Jane and Carmel had to struggle to keep their heads above water and to earn a living for themselves and their children on the little farm. Carmel became increasingly despondent over their deplorable financial situation and his mother's action. Then, a little less than a year and a half after his mother's death, on October 15, 1883, he did the unthinkable by committing suicide.

As a result of Carmel's death, Sarah Jane was left with three fatherless young children. Joseph was a mere three months and eight days old, Mabel was a little over four years of age and the eldest, my grandmother, was only seven and half. Sarah Jane had Carmel interred in the Vassar Riverside Cemetery and then turned to the task of providing for her family and herself. With the help of her relatives and neighbors, she continued to run the farm and even found the time to hire herself out to some of the locals for seasonal housework.

The little family eked out a living for a period of nearly four years before Sarah Jane met a man who was destined to become her second husband. He was Willie H. Jaeger and though various family members have attempted to find information about his background, none has been able to do so. The man seems to have just appeared on the Michigan scene as if by magic.

Sarah Jane and Willie were wed on February 2, 1887. She entered the marriage with the fervent hope that part of her family burden thus would be eased. Eleven months after their wedding a son was born to their union. The couple named him John Wesley Jaeger and he joined the family on January 5, 1888. It didn't take very long for Sarah Jane to learn that her new husband had a problem—he was a drinker. Not only was he an alcoholic but he was a mean drunk as well. On his binges he was both verbally and physically abusive to Sarah Jane and also to the children.

Following the old adage, "Hope springs eternal in the human breast," Sarah Jane put up with Willie's abuse for a few years after their son was born. However, she came to the sad realization that he was not going to change and that it was up to her to remove herself and the children from a very dangerous situation. Reluctantly she filed for divorce on the grounds of drunkenness and cruelty and within the year it was granted. Willie seems to have gone away willingly, but he still had one last cruelty to inflict upon his then ex-wife. When he left the area, he took young John Wesley with him and none of the family ever heard from either of them again.

Not only was Sarah Jane once again the sole breadwinner for her family but she had suffered the loss of her youngest child as well. A photograph taken in 1891 of the pupils and teacher of Tuscola Center School, which the children attended, clearly shows how needy the family must have been at the time. Sarah Jane's son, Joseph, eight years old, is one of only four students in the photo without shoes.

Sarah Jane struggled to earn a living for her family by continuing to run the farm after her divorce. She still augmented its income by finding work wherever she could in the neighborhood. The marriage of her eldest daughter, Maude, in 1893 relieved Sarah Jane's burden somewhat because it meant there was one less mouth to feed. Maude, who was to become my maternal grandmother, was seventeen years old at the time. She and her new husband, Jacob Franklin Williamson, moved to his hometown of Findlay, Ohio to start their family.

In 1898, Sarah Jane heard about a job opening of a permanent nature in Port Huron, Michigan, and thought her prayers had been answered. Because that city was situated about ninety miles distant from Vassar, she took a train for the job interview. Joseph, her fifteen year old son, accompanied her on the trip. When they arrived at their destination, Sarah Jane hired a "hack" (a horse-drawn buggy used as a taxi) for the ride to the hotel where they planned to stay. At the hotel Joseph dismounted from the hack and Sarah Jane started to follow suit. Just as she did so, the horse lunged forward and the buggy's movement violently knocked her to the pavement. Her arm was severely fractured in the vain attempt to break her fall before hitting the cement. Sarah Jane was carried to the hotel where she was put to bed and a doctor was summoned.

A year previous to that my grandparents had moved back to Vassar from Findlay, Ohio in order for Grandfather Williamson to find work. By the time of the accident they already had four children all under the age of five and the youngest, Lettie, was only a few months old. Grandmother received a telegram describing her mother's condition and immediately took the train to Port Huron. She would serve as nurse until Sarah Jane became well enough for the return trip. However, that was not to happen. One of the lacerations on Sarah Jane's arm became infected with gangrene and formed an abscess. The poison spread throughout her body and less than two weeks later, on January 11, 1899, she died.

My grandmother was left with the doleful task of bringing her younger brother and the body of her mother on the train back to Vassar. The ill-fated Sarah Jane was laid to rest next to her first husband, Carmel, in the cemetery overlooking the Cass River. Her unhappy and unlucky short life was at an end.

Carmel Townsend's Parents
Ruth (White) Townsend &
Aziel Townsend

Carmel Townsend &
Sarah Jane (Shook) Townsend
(Infant is Maude Townsend)

Carmel & Sarah Jane Townsend's
Children
(L to R) Mabel, Maude & Joseph

# CHAPTER 8

## COVERED WAGON WEST

My great uncle, Joe, along with two young friends, embarked on a feat in 1910 which set the three of them apart from most other people at the time. In that era, when the general populace had little chance for or interest in far flung travels, they proved themselves to be of a different sort. The trio not only built, but drove a covered wagon from Vassar, Michigan to central Oregon—a distance of twenty-three hundred miles.

What was their motivation for such a long trek? Perhaps it was to break out of their humdrum existence and to put a little adventure into their lives. It could have been merely a desire to see "far away places with strange sounding names" as the old popular song implied. Whatever did provide the impetus for such an undertaking must have been rather compelling because of the effort it entailed. As a result of their accomplishment Joseph's existence changed completely because, from that date on, he made Oregon his home. Only twice did he return to visit his family members in Michigan before he died nearly forty years later.

Joseph Dewain Townsend, or "Uncle Joe," as he was known in the family, was my maternal grandmother's youngest sibling. He was born on July 5, 1883 shortly after his father, Carmel Townsend, learned that he had been disinherited by his own mother. Unfortunately that meant that he would receive nothing from her large estate. The grim news put Carmel into a deep depression from which he never recovered. His despondency worsened and eventually it led to his suicide on October 15<sup>th</sup> of that same year. At the time of his father's death, Joseph was only three months and eight days old.

Over the next two decades, Joseph's bereft family struggled through financial hardship and an almost unbelievable number of other tragedies. They included a disastrous second marriage by Sarah Jane, Joseph's mother, a resulting unpleasant divorce, the loss of a younger half brother and finally Sarah Jane's untimely death when young Joseph was only fifteen years old. (See the chapter titled "Ill-Fated Sarah Jane Shook.")

During the rest of Joseph's teenage years he lived with various relatives in Vassar. He spent some time with his sister, Maude, and her family—they were my Williamson grandparents—and also with his maternal aunt, Elsie Ann, and her husband, Eugene Morse. The Morse family included seven children who were near Joseph's age and he grew to be very close to them.

Perry Morse and Joseph, who were three years apart in age, became very good friends—in fact, they could be called "best buddies." The friendship continued even after Perry married a local girl named Lillie. All three of them were avid readers and especially enjoyed stories about the Far West. Those tales stirred their adventurous spirits and abetted a shared desire to explore beyond Michigan's borders. In the course of many excited conversations the trio eventually hatched the idea that together they could build a covered wagon. Then, with it as transportation, they could actually visit the romantic West about which they had read so much.

Once the decision had been made to go, the young people immediately set to work and within a year had built a Conestoga-type covered wagon, purchased a horse to pull it, collected supplies needed en route and were ready to begin their long trek. When they started out from Vassar in the spring of 1910, Joseph was twenty-seven and Perry was thirty and all were eager to begin the adventure of their lives. Their families, on the other hand, were not convinced that the trip was a good idea. However, no amount of coaxing or predictions of dire consequences could dissuade the three of them from their remarkable venture.

I have no information about the more than two thousand mile trip or the hardships they endured while heading west, but I'm certain they were legion. Suffice it to say that they arrived relatively unscathed in the wilds of central Oregon that fall. Perhaps the narrow confines of the covered wagon had caused a little too much "togetherness" en route because from there they went different ways. Joseph remained in Oregon and Perry and Lillie went on to California and stayed there for a time. Eventually the couple separated and Perry came back to Michigan again.

Joseph explored and prospected along the McKenzie River in central western Oregon and eventually staked a claim in a cinnabar mine. Cinnabar is a heavy compound of mercury and sulfur and is the most important ore in the production of mercury. It is not clear how successful Joseph was, but apparently he did make some profit. Eventually he homesteaded near the central Oregon town of Prineville, situated on the Crooked River. His property backed up to a railroad that ran along Ocheco Creek. There he built a two-story house with an attached greenhouse and separate workshop where he could putter at his various interests.

For a time Joseph worked as the grave digger for the local cemetery and made a hobby of collecting an assortment of artifacts, minerals and soil samples he dug up—originally from prospecting but later from grave digging. After building an apartment for his own use connected to the workshop, he rented the house to tenants. Later Joseph added another room which my Curtis cousins, who lived with him for a while, called "the laboratory" because it held all the treasures from his years of collecting. After Joseph's death the cousins spent weeks exploring the jam-packed laboratory with its many cabinets and numerous shelves filled to overflowing with items he found interesting and collectable.

Joseph also loved books so he added a library to the suite of rooms. Eventually its walls were filled from top to bottom with books and magazines. Even the floor was covered with more boxes of books. My brother, Laurel, tells me that he still owns a ten volume set from Joseph's collection which he bought at the estate sale after Joseph died. It is The Works of Edgar Allan Poe, published in 1904.

Uncle Joe, a perennial bachelor, was generous to a fault. Not only did he take in relatives who were in need of a place to stay but he did the same for friends as well. One of those friends, a mechanic who was having trouble supporting his family, is a good case in point. Joe built a garage attached to his library and let the mechanic use it to earn his living. Later he built another house on the property and invited the man and his family to live there.

According to the recollections of my mother's last remaining first cousin, Evelyn Gratsch, Joseph visited Michigan once when she was very young. Evelyn was Joseph's niece and she remembered that he came to visit her mother, Mabel Palmer who was his older sister. Evelyn was born in 1920, therefore the visit must have been around 1925 or 1926.

About twenty years later, in 1946, when Joseph was sixty-three years old, he made his second return trip to Michigan. At the time he was nearly eligible for Social Security benefits but needed his birth certificate for verification of his age. My brother, Laurel, recalls that because the Tuscola County Court House in Caro had burned down and all the older birth records were destroyed, getting a birth certificate had become a complicated process. It was necessary for an applicant to appear in person and provide witnesses who would attest to the birth. That bureaucratic snag gave Joseph the opportunity for a visit with his family members whom he hadn't seen in nearly two decades. The reunion was a happy event and he spent several weeks becoming re-acquainted with the older relatives and meeting the younger set, including my cousins and me, for the first time.

It is fortunate that Joseph made the trip back to see the family when he did because he passed away at his Prineville home less than two years later on March 20, 1948. Ironically his only remaining sister, my Great Aunt Mabel, died only fifteen days after he did. Their other sibling, my Grandmother Williamson, had passed away six years earlier in 1942.

My mother's youngest sister, Marguerite Curtis, and her family were living with Uncle Joe in Prineville at the time of his death. Marguerite was his nearest relative in the area (she was his niece) and therefore took on the formidable task of settling his estate and dispersing his belongings as well as the voluminous collections. She organized the estate sale where my brother bought the Edgar Allan Poe volumes.

Joseph Townsend
Lillie Morse & Perry Morse
(Lillie & Perry seated on wagon)

Joseph Townsend (right)
(Prospecting on the McKenzie
River in west central Oregon)

# CHAPTER 9

## "UNCLE"

One of my favorite relatives when I was a child was someone my mother always referred to simply as "Uncle." Her reason for calling him that was because he was the only one of her two uncles with whom she had any contact. Her mother's only brother, Joseph Townsend, lived most of his adult life in Oregon so she didn't know him at all. But Levi, her father's only brother, lived next door to the house in Vassar where she was born and raised. His residence was a two-room house located just east of my grandparents' home on Wightman Street.

Though Uncle was deaf and mute—he could only make squeaks and guttural noises—in his own inimitable way he was able to communicate his wants and needs to the rest of the family. I was a mere six years old when he passed away but had already learned to know him well. He was always a kind, generous and jolly character whom I enjoyed seeing when I visited my grandparents next door.

Levi Marshall Williamson was born in Findlay, Ohio in the summer of 1861 just a few months after the first shots of the Civil War were fired at Fort Sumter in South Carolina. He was the eldest son of Abraham and Almira Williamson and had been named after both of his grandfathers, Dr. Levi Williamson and Levi Marshall Miller. Almira, Levi's mother, was of hardy Pennsylvania Dutch stock with German names like Alspach and Fuhr in her background. The family lived in a German-speaking neighborhood in Findlay so Levi began life as a bi-lingual child.

In 1865, when Levi was four years old, he and his mother went on a trip to Gagetown, Michigan in order to visit his carpenter father who was spending the summer there building a new home for his parents. Abraham's father and stepmother, Levi and Agnes Williamson, had homesteaded in the Thumb area of Michigan in 1863. To make the trip, Almira and young Levi traveled by boat from Ohio through Lake Erie, up the Detroit River to Lake St. Clair, north on the St. Clair River to Lake Huron and finally docked at Bay City, Michigan. There they were met by Levi's Grandfather Williamson, and the trio traveled by ox cart for the last thirty mile leg of the trip to Gagetown.

While aboard the ship, Levi was overcome with a massive fever. Paralysis set in and he lost control of his arms and legs. We now know that he had contracted the dreaded disease, Poliomyelitis or Infantile Paralysis, as it was once known. In addition to causing temporary paralysis of Levi's arms and legs, the disease did damage to his brain stem which affected his speech and hearing as well. His grandfather, who was a doctor, prescribed the application of hot, moist cloths to Levi's arms and legs and twenty four hour manipulation of his limbs. The treatment was successful in the sense that it averted permanent paralysis but a failure in another sense because Levi was left without the ability to hear or speak.

Levi later attended the Michigan School for the Deaf in Flint, Michigan as a boarding student and completed his education through the eighth grade. His parents and younger brother (who would become my maternal grandfather) moved to Vassar about thirty miles north of Flint to be nearer the school and Levi's father, Abraham, found work as a carpenter there. The Williamsons lived in Vassar for the rest of their lives.

While enrolled at the school for the deaf, Levi learned sign language in addition to sewing and cooking. He also was taught two occupational skills—shoe repairing and rug weaving. As an adult he earned his living for a number of years as a cobbler (shoe repairman) in the tiny clapboard house he built in Vassar on property adjacent to my grandparents' home. Levi remained a bachelor who made his own meals and did his own housekeeping and laundry throughout his long life.

Eventually Levi's chosen profession became debilitating for him. The constant pounding as he held the shoes on his lap while repairing them, injured his knees and Levi began to have difficulty walking. Undaunted, he turned to the other skill he had been taught and took up rug weaving. Levi purchased a loom and put out a hand-made sign stating:

# CARPET WEAVING

## Levi M. Williamson

He attached the sign just above the front door of his tiny house and from that point on was open for business. Rug weaving occupied Levi for the balance of his life.

By the time I came into the family Levi's weaving enterprise had outgrown his house and had been moved to a former chicken coop which he had remodeled into a weaving shop. I recall being fascinated by watching him sitting at the loom using a foot pedal to raise and lower the harnesses holding the warp (vertical strings) and throwing the shuttle with the woof (horizontal strips of cloth) across the machine through the warp shed. After each throw of the shuttle, he would send the beater crashing down to tighten the weave.

Levi made what were called "rag rugs" in a wide variety of linear patterns. The "rags" were narrow pieces of cloth cut from worn-out clothing and sewn together end to end into long strips. All of the family members saved their old clothing for him to use as raw material for his enterprise. Levi could vary both the length and the width of the different rugs and, in addition, he formed striped patterns by grouping like colors together with contrasting colors next to them. I have childish memories of seeing examples of his rug weaving artistry in nearly every room in our house. In fact, some of Levi's rugs still remain in the family today, nearly seventy years after his death.

For the last twenty-five years of his life, Levi carried a white scar across his nose. I often wondered what caused the blemish but didn't find out until years later. It seems that he was splitting wood too near an outdoor clothes line. On one of the back swings his ax caught the clothes line and the wire came down across his nose, nearly slicing it in two. Levi was taken to the family doctor who stitched him back together. The bandage he wore until it healed was so large that he was unable to wear his glasses. Of course, the wound left an ugly scar in its wake and it served as a constant reminder of his foolishness on that occasion.

In spite of his speaking and hearing handicaps, Levi gave every indication that he thoroughly enjoyed being a part of the family and that he led a happy and fulfilling life. At Christmas time he played Santa Clause for his nieces and nephews next door and even created an appropriate red costume for the occasion. On weekends he was a regular guest at my grandparents' home for Sunday dinners and occasionally returned the invitation. However his sister-in-law, my Grandmother, was wary of letting her family eat in his home because she felt that his household cleanliness and sanitation were rather suspect.

Levi died in his little house on Wightman Street in 1938 at the age of seventy-six and a half. His passing left a void in the Williamson family that was hard to fill. Even today, when I pass the house, my thoughts turn to my kindly, generous and jolly kinsman who once occupied it.

Levi Marshall Williamson
(With woven rug display in front
of his home in Vassar)

Uncle's rug weaving shop
(Converted from a chicken coop)

Levi Marshall Williamson
(1861 – 1938)

# CHAPTER 10

## A FAMILY VISIT ON THE CASS RIVER

The lazy Cass River flowed through Vassar about a half mile from the house where my mother and her siblings were born and raised. The river figured prominently in the history of the area from the time of Vassar's founding. Early on a dam had been built across its width to provide power for running grist mills and other river-side enterprises. In addition, through the decades, thousands of board feet of lumber had been floated along its waterway en route to sawmills downriver.

The Cass provided Vassar residents with recreational opportunities as well. It was shallow and slow-moving enough in summer that it was deemed safe for swimming and one section of the river near the south end of town actually had a sandy beach. My mother remembers that area, which they dubbed "Sandy," as being her family's favorite area for swimming. During the winter time the Cass River's ice-covered surface also provided a skating arena for townspeople. Some hearty individuals even sawed through the frozen surface to try their luck at ice fishing or spearing through the resulting holes.

Nearly every day during the three other seasons one could see both children and adults fishing from its banks

When my mother and her brothers and sisters were young, their family was poor and usually had no automobile. The Cass River occasionally served their transportation needs. Mother's father, Jacob Franklin Williamson, who had many talents, also proved that he was an artist in woodworking. One of Grandfather's more noteworthy carpentry projects was to build a large rowboat for the family's use. They spent much time on the Cass River in the boat and usually enjoyed it thoroughly.

However, one of their river excursions nearly ended in tragedy.

On a Sunday morning early in the summer of 1912, when Mother was just under three years old, her parents and several of the younger children, including Bob, who was a baby, boated downriver. They followed the river's languid course about five or six miles in a generally southwest direction and planned to enjoy an early afternoon dinner with Mother's Aunt Mabel and her family. Mabel (Townsend) Palmer was Grandmother Williamson's only sister. She, with her husband Edward Palmer and their children, lived on a farm near the Cass about a mile north of the Village of Tuscola. En route the warm summer sun shone through the trees bordering the meandering river and cast dappled shadows on the water as they made their way that happy day.

The trip downriver to visit the Palmer's farm was pleasant and uneventful. While spending the next few hours together the two families enjoyed chatting with one another and having a reunion dinner. By the time the

Williamsons were ready to head back to Vassar, the sun had dropped low in the west. That return trip was noticeably slower because rowing the boat upstream proved to be much more difficult.

Half way home, when dusk had overtaken them, they came to a sand bar in the river which effectively halted their progress. To solve the problem, Grandfather Williamson removed his shoes, rolled up his pant legs and stepped out of the boat to pull it across the sand bar. While he was doing that the boat struck a stone which upset its balance and caused it to lurch violently to one side. Grandmother Williamson shrieked as the baby was wrenched from her grasp and tossed into the river. Many years later Mother described the scene in her memoirs,

*"Mama screamed, Papa rushed back, pulling the baby, coughing and dripping from the water. I can see him now, looking for all the world like a drowned rat."*

Fortunately the infant had not been thrown against a rock in the river. Though water-drenched, gasping and sputtering, he was otherwise uninjured. Luck was with the family that day because the frightening experience could have had much more tragic consequences. Following that excitement the family made its way back home to Vassar with no further incidents.

Mother long remembered the horror of that river trip which took all the fun out of boating for her for years to come. In spite of her fear of water craft, I feel that Mother probably was the most "at ease" person whom I have ever seen in water while swimming. She could float comfortably in a pool or lake and often would lie there for long periods of time without moving her limbs to stay afloat. When I try to do the same thing, invariably my feet and legs sink first and I end up in the water instead of on it. Apparently Mother possessed innate buoyancy that I do not share.

Edward & Mabel Palmer & 3
eldest children (Ruth, Roy, Leah)
On their farm near the Cass River

Williamson & Palmer Families
(1920)

# CHAPTER 11

## THE FATEFUL MEETING ON THE STAIRS

On a sunny, clear day in the early fall of 1915, twenty-three year old Frank Seney first saw his future wife. The incident occurred while he was walking home from the train station in his hometown of Vassar, Michigan. Frank had just gotten off the eastbound train returning from an adventurous few months spent working the grain harvest in the American West with his older brother, Sam. That was the first time he had ever been out of the state of Michigan, and Frank was eagerly looking forward to seeing his parents again.

The fall air was cool and crisp and the late afternoon sunlight dappled the colorful autumn foliage as Frank hurried along South Main Street. A couple of blocks from the business district he turned west on a plank sidewalk. The walkway bordered Saginaw Street at the base of the sharp rise that effectively divided Vassar into two parts, both physically and economically. Generally the wealthier set lived at the top and the rest at its base nearer the river. The two areas were referred to as "The Hill" and "Below the Hill."

In the late 1800s the city fathers built a wooden stairway along Saginaw Street to make it easier for pedestrians to scale the steep rise to the top of the hill. That structure was soon dubbed "The Golden Stairs" and it was bordered on the south by tall evergreen trees. Frank approached the steps and began the ascent. Idly, he glanced up the stairway and noticed a young lady coming toward him on the way down. He didn't recognize her but was immediately smitten with her beauty. He realized at once that he wished to meet her. "What excuse can I use to start a conversation with her?" Frank asked himself frantically.

By the time the young people met near the center of the stairway, Frank solved his problem. His conversational opening wasn't very original but it served his purpose. He politely tipped his hat and said, "Pardon me, but do you know where the Seney family lives?" The young lady nodded and explained that their house was on Wilmot Street immediately behind where her family lived. Then the two continued their separate ways. After Frank had gained the top of the stairs, he turned and took a second and longer look at the lovely apparition he had just met. In doing so he caught her covertly glancing up to take another peek at him as well. "Ah hah!" he thought, "Not only do I find her attractive but she is interested in me too!"

Very self-satisfied, Frank turned away and continued on his way home. The elder Seneys—Sam and Agnes, along with Frank and their other two sons, Sam, Jr., and Bill—lived in a small house a few blocks west of the stairway. Wilmot was one of the shortest streets in town as it began at West Street and ended only two short blocks from there at the edge of Wightman's Woods. Frank entered the home and found his mother in the lean-to kitchen preparing dinner for the family. His mother greeted him effusively. After barely saying hello to her

Frank exclaimed, "Guess what, Mother! I've just met the most beautiful girl in the world and I'm going to marry her!" "That's nice, Frank." Agnes replied offhandedly. She was used to his sudden binges of excitement and assumed this was just another of those.

Frank, however, soon proved his mother wrong. In the next few days he somehow wangled more visits with my Aunt Lulu Williamson—the lady on the stairway—and they were married a little less than a year from the day they first saw one another. The young couple bought a small house on West Street just around the corner from Frank's parents' home and there they raised a family of four sons and one daughter.

Frank held several different jobs in the Vassar area but during most of his working career, he was employed at the Vassar Post Office. Only after suffering a debilitating stroke in his mid sixties did he agree to retirement. Aunt Lulu was not only a beautiful woman but a successful homemaker, a wonderful mother and, in her advanced years, a kind and loving grandmother and great-grandmother as well. One of her daughters-in-law, Bonnie Seney, gave her the ultimate compliment when she told me that Aunt Lulu was "the perfect mother-in-law."

Aunt Lulu and Uncle Frank came within six months of celebrating their sixtieth wedding anniversary when he died in 1971. Aunt Lulu lived for another twelve years before passing away at the age of eighty-six in 1983. I recall being part of the crowd attending her funeral. The many mourners there filled the large sanctuary in the Vassar Baptist Church to overflow capacity.

Today, Frank and Lulu Seney's descendants number in the hundreds and they provide a living tribute to the couple's chance meeting in 1915 on The Golden Stairs in Vassar.

Frank J. Seney &
Lulu (Williamson) Seney
(Wedding Photo – 1916)

The Golden Stairs
Vassar, Michigan
(about 1910)

# CHAPTER 12

## THE WILLIAMSON SISTERS

My mother, Ernestine (Williamson) Davis, had four brothers and six sisters. Her male siblings all died relatively young. The first-born son, Franklin Pierce, died shortly before his twenty-third birthday, William Joseph died at twenty, Paul Lester lived longer than any of his brothers and died at fifty-six and the youngest, Robert Townsend, passed away at the age of forty-four. Except for one, the girls in the Williamson family had long lives. That one exception to the rule was Dorothy C. who died when she was less than a year old.

Mother's oldest sister was Mamie. She was born in the summer of 1894 and throughout her life she played big sister to all the others. One of her first jobs was working for her dad in his photography studio above a drugstore on the corner of Main street and Huron Avenue in Vassar's downtown. Mamie married George Sinclair in 1915 and their only child, Edgar Richard (Dick) was born a year later. That marriage was short lived, however, because George contracted Tuberculosis and succumbed to the disease in April of 1917 when his son was about a year old.

After her husband's death, Mamie moved to the Detroit area to find work. There she met the man who would become her second husband. He was William (Bill) Gobb whom she wed in 1919 when she was twenty five and he was thirty-five. Bill worked for the railroad his entire career. One child, Virginia Mary, was born to that union which lasted sixty-two years and only ended with Mamie's death in 1981 just six days before her eighty-seventh birthday. Bill followed her only a few months later shortly after his ninety-seventh birthday.

Mamie was the only Williamson sister who lived in or near a large city. Early in their married life she and Bill had a home built in the Detroit suburb of Wyandotte. I remember that she had one cardinal rule for interior decoration and time after time I have heard her say this. "I like any wall color in my house as long as it is green." True to her credo, every room in the Wyandotte home <u>was</u> some shade of green. Mamie carried that same color scheme to the grounds of their house where she used her talented "green thumb" for landscaping as well as flower and vegetable gardening.

The next eldest Williamson sister was Lulu Gustina. (I have often wondered what she thought about her middle name, but never had the temerity to ask her.) Lulu was born in the winter of 1896 in Findlay, Ohio where the Williamsons were living when the first three of their eleven children were born. She was attractive and photogenic as a young lady and often the subject of her photographer father's pictures.

Lulu married Frank Seney of Vassar when she was twenty. (For the story of how they met, see "The Fateful Meeting on the Stairs".) They had four sons, James, Lloyd, Gene and Glenn. When the youngest of their sons, Glenn, was sixteen years old, Lulu presented them with a baby sister, Frances. She was nearly forty-six at the time.

In the summer of 1956, Frank Seney at the age of sixty-five, suffered a debilitating stroke which left him unable to work and needing a great deal of personal care. Lulu provided that care for fifteen years and never seemed to complain about being saddled with the twenty-four hour duty. Frank was sometimes frustrated with his inability to do much and consequently lashed out at anyone within reach. Lulu bore that with her usual equanimity. In her later years, Lulu reminded me of her own mother, who I felt was the perfect grandmother to my siblings, my cousins and me. Frank died in February of 1971 but Lulu lived for another twelve years and passed away in the fall of 1983. At the time of her death, Lulu had seventeen grandchildren and many, many great grandchildren.

Violette May (Lettie) was the next Williamson sister in age. She was born in the winter of 1898 only a little over a year prior to the turn of the century. Lettie had dimples all her life and as a young lady, like her older sister, Lulu, was often photographed by her father, Jacob Franklin Williamson. Lettie married Frank Seney's elder brother, Sam. Thus two of the Williamson sisters married Seney brothers.

Lettie and Sam never had any children during their marriage. They lived in a small house on West Street in Vassar for much of their wedded life. Lettie raised a large garden on the property and kept her house in immaculate order. I remember visiting there and observing her collection of <u>National Geographic</u> magazines arranged <u>in order</u> according to date of issue and perfectly aligned with one another on the shelves of her book case.

Lettie loved to sing and she and Sam attended the Vassar Baptist Church when I was in high school. I recall sitting near them in the pews and hearing her voice over the others. What made her singing so distinctive was her vibrato. It almost sounded as though she were gargling the hymns. Nonetheless she was always perfectly in tune.

Lettie passed away in 1985 at the age of eighty-six, a few years after her husband. Though the residence has been completely remodeled and looks quite different from when they lived there, I still think of Sam and Lettie each time I pass their little house on West Street in Vassar.

Among the Williamson sisters who lived to adulthood, Florence Lillian was the next younger after Lettie. (Dorothy, who was born between the two, died as an infant.) Florence was born in March of 1905 at the Williamson home on Wightman Street in Vassar. My mother told me that, as a teenager, Florence often cared for her three younger siblings because her mother, my grandmother Williamson, suffered ill health during much of that period of time.

Eighteen year old Florence married Howard Baldwin from Tuscola in the summer of 1923. He was twenty-five at the time and worked at a General Motors automobile manufacturing plant in Flint, Michigan. They were a handsome couple even though she was several inches taller than he. Florence was a superb dressmaker and made and altered clothing for many of her friends, relatives and neighbors. I recall that she had a dress form standing next to her sewing machine which was shaped like her daughter's torso. Florence used the form to make Betty's clothing long after she left home for college and later marriage. I found it totally fascinating that Florence would often refer to the thing as "Betty."

Betty Marie Baldwin, Howard and Florence's eldest child, was born in 1924. Their second and last child, Don Mervin, was born three years later. The Baldwins lived in Tuscola until Betty and Don were through college and then they had a new home built north of the village on Frankenmuth Road.

Florence was a woman of many talents. Besides tailoring and dressmaking she wall- papered and painted, did minor carpentry, plus other household maintenance. She could upholster and re-finish furniture, was a marvelous cook, and kept an immaculate house. One time when I was furnishing one of my first apartments, I purchased an old, tattered studio couch. Florence came to my rescue and re-upholstered it for me. I must admit that hers and my mother's interest in and zest for building and remodeling inspired me along those same lines.

Howard died in 1968 at the age of seventy, but Florence outlived him by more than a quarter of a century. She moved to Traverse City for her last years and attained the ripe old age of eighty-nine before passing away.

My mother, Ernestine Vere, was the next to the youngest of the Williamson sisters. She was born on July first in 1909. Mother was the studious sort who loved to read and to write; therefore she excelled in schoolwork. She was plagued all her life with being extremely shy. In fact, during her final year of high school she purposely cut back on her studies simply because she was petrified at the thought of having to give either the valedictory or the salutatory address before the graduation audience. Through her successful machinations she ended up third in her 1928 graduating class and avoided doing any speechmaking.

Ernestine married Dayton Davis from Tuscola on the Fourth of July in 1929. Their wedding ceremony was performed in the flower garden behind her parent's home on Wightman Street in Vassar. After a week-long honeymoon spent camping in Michigan's Upper Peninsula, they settled in Tuscola. Within a year they made the down payment on a seventy-seven acre farm just north of the village and moved there before my brother, Laurel was born in 1930.

I followed Laurel into the family in 1932, my sister Joanne came along in 1934 and Dan completed the family in 1936. Mother, like her sisters, was a multi-talented person. She was a wonderful cook, a fine seamstress, a fascinating storyteller, an accomplished artist, an inspired interior decorator, a noteworthy writer and a person who loved mathematics. If she had one failing it was that she disliked housework. I guess no one is totally perfect!

Mother lived about two months after her eighty-sixth birthday and passed away in 1995. Dad outlived her by nearly seven years and died in February of 2002 at the age of ninety-four and a half.

Marguerite Eleanor was the youngest of the Williamson sisters and she was born in the fall of 1915. She probably suffered more heartache than any of her older sisters throughout her lifetime. At the age of eighteen Marguerite had a child, Nancy Lou, whom the family encouraged her to give up for adoption. She maintained some contact with her daughter through the years but it wasn't until Nancy was an adult that they became close.

Marguerite married Russell Curtis in 1938 and they had four children—Richard (Dick), born in 1939, Maralee, in 1940, Philip, in 1942 and Jackie, in 1943. Their third child, Philip, only lived for about two years and died as a result of a tumor. When the children were small, the family moved to Prineville, Oregon where Marguerite's uncle, Joseph Townsend, lived. Times were hard, jobs were scarce and the marriage eventually fell apart. Marguerite and the children came back to Michigan where she earned a living by being a live-in housekeeper for widowers in the Vassar area.

Marguerite eventually married Clinton Hollister, one of the widowers for whom she kept house. They lived at his home near North Lake, Michigan and spent many winters in Florida. He died in 1995 and she followed him a little over a year later in 1996 at the age of eighty. Her only remaining son, Dick, predeceased her by about six months.

When the Williamson sisters were among crowds in any type of public gathering, they were rather shy people. However, that shyness left them when they assembled in family get-togethers—one of their favorite forms of entertainment. How well I remember the heightened noise level and the general "joy of living" all of them exhibited at family reunions. Their respective husbands, in self defense, often moved to other parts of the house or outside in order to make themselves heard above the happy din.

The sisters were wholesome and talented ladies who left a legacy of heirs numbering in the hundreds.

Lulu Gustina Williamson
(1896 – 1983)

Mamie Irene Williamson
(1894 – 1981

Violette May (Lettie) Williamson
(1898 – 1985)

The Williamson Sisters – 1970
Standing (L to R) Lulu, Ernestine, Mamie, Lettie
Seated (L to R) Marguerite, Florence

## CHAPTER 13

## A TRAGIC YEAR FOR THE FAMILY

The year 1920 was a most unhappy one for my mother's family. In February the eldest son in the family died of influenza and only a short four months later the second eldest male succumbed to the lethal effects of gas warfare in World War I. The two deaths, so close to one another, profoundly shocked the entire family.

Franklin Pierce Williamson was born on February 16, 1897, the third child, but the first son of my maternal grandparents, Jacob Franklin and Maude Dette Williamson. Like his two older sisters, his birth took place at the family's home in Findlay, Ohio. Pierce, as he was always known, was given both names of the fourteenth president of the United States, Franklin Pierce, and, coincidentally, Franklin also was his father's middle name. When Pierce was about a year old the family moved to Vassar, Michigan, his mother's hometown. Grandfather Williamson had experienced difficulty earning a living in Ohio and made the move to Michigan in an attempt to find more lucrative employment.

Pierce's birth was followed closely by that of his sister, Violette May in 1898, and by his brother, William in 1899. That second son, who went by the nickname, Bill, was born eleven days before Christmas of that year, and was given an old and respected Williamson name. His great great grandfather was named William, as was one of his great uncles and also one of his great great uncles. For Bill's middle name his parents chose Joseph, in honor of his mother's grandfather, Joseph Shook. Eventually six more children joined the Williamson Family for a grand total of eleven.

Mother wrote in her memoirs that her large family was a happy one. They were poor but seemed unaware of it at the time. Both Pierce and Bill played the roles of big brothers for their younger siblings. The children grew up in a house at the end of Wightman Street on the southern edge of Vassar, adjacent to Wightman Woods. The woods presented the children with many opportunities for exploration and play. Also their home was within a half mile of the Cass River which added to their year round recreation.

In April, 1917, the United States Congress declared war on Germany, thus entering World War I. The government quickly adopted a selective service act which required all men between the ages of twenty-one and thirty to register for the draft. Soon eye-catching Uncle Sam posters appeared almost everywhere stating unequivocally "I WANT YOU!" Bill Williamson, who was only seventeen at the time, but always the adventurous sort, decided to answer his country's call and join the army. One minor problem presented itself—his age. The military was only accepting recruits who were eighteen or older. Undaunted, Bill followed in the footsteps of his namesake and maternal great grandfather,

Joseph Shook—he lied his age. (See the chapter called "A Warrior in the Family.")

After a short army basic training at Ft. Bliss, Texas, Bill found himself on a troop ship crossing the Atlantic to Europe. During the next year he saw action with the American Expeditionary Forces in the trenches of France. Though Germany was the first to use chemicals as a weapon during that war, nevertheless they were employed by both the Allies and the Central Powers. Bill's unit was one of those that came under a German gas attack. My mother claimed that her "devil-may-care" elder brother gave his gas mask to a fellow soldier who didn't have one and therefore took the brunt of the chemical attack without the necessary protection. The gas did not kill him immediately but it did affect him severely. He became extremely ill and was sent back to the United States for treatment at a military hospital in Camp Sherman, Ohio.

During the war, Pierce Williamson took his position of "older brother" to his siblings very seriously. Still in his early twenties, he continued to live in the Williamson home on Wightman Street because he was unmarried. To help augment the family income he accepted a job with the Pere Marquette Railroad that ran through Vassar. He worked as a member of the railroad's paint gang and regularly brought his wages home for the good of all.

World War I wasn't the only killer of millions of people in Europe during 1918 and 1919. The other culprit was the Spanish Influenza. The war promoted the spread of the dreaded disease because people moved around more than usual and thus became exposed to the virus. It is likely that it crossed the ocean from Europe to North America with returning American troops and it wreaked havoc on the populations of both continents. In all, the pandemic is reported to have killed twenty million people. Influenza causes most of its deaths because it leaves patients in a vulnerable state and subjects them to opportunistic diseases such as pneumonia, bronchitis, plus mastoid and sinus infections.

The Williamson family was not spared from the serious effects of the Spanish Influenza. According to

Mother's memoirs, first her elder sister, Lettie who was married and lived nearby, came down with the disease. Before she was fully recovered, Florence was stricken. She was only fifteen and still living at the Williamson home. From her the virus spread to other family members. The only person in the household to escape was Grandfather Williamson, who claimed that he avoided the disease with a home remedy concocted of lemon juice and cream of tarter.

One day in early February of 1920, when the rest of the household was recovering nicely, Pierce came home from his job with the railroad paint gang, flushed and feeling ill. He reported that every member of the gang was also sick—in fact one of them already had died from the disease. Pierce was put to bed and the overworked family doctor was summoned. He was able to do little for the young man. Pierce was violently ill and even delirious during the short week that he lasted. Neighbors and family members kept a twenty-four hour vigil at his bedside, but to no avail. He expired during the night of February 10th with his mother and father at his side. Pierce was only six days short of his twenty-third birthday.

Pierce's funeral was a private family affair because the Williamson house was under strict quarantine. Nonetheless Bill was called home from the army hospital in Ohio where he was under treatment for the effects of the poison gas. While on leave from the hospital Bill appeared to be recovering, but did have a bad cough due to the severe damage done to his lungs. He returned to the hospital in Ohio immediately after the funeral. Later that spring, his family was notified that his condition had worsened and Grandmother Williamson traveled there by train to be with him. While she was in Ohio, he seemed to rally somewhat so she returned to Vassar. That rally, however, was of short duration because soon she was notified that he was near death. She rushed back to the hospital and was there at his deathbed on the eighteenth of June, 1920, only four months and eight days after his brother passed away. Bill was six months short of reaching twenty-one when he died.

Grandmother Williamson had the sad task of bringing the body of her second son back on the train when she returned to Vassar. Consequently, the Williamson family home was the scene of yet another funeral within only a half year span of time. Fortunately there were no further deaths in the family for the next two decades.

Bill Williamson (on left)
(1899 – 1920)
France – World War I

Pierce Williamson
(1897 – 1920)

# THE DAVIS, JOHNSON & ROSENCRANTS FAMILIES

# CHAPTER 14

# ROLE PLAYING AT PLIMOTH PLANTATION

During the summer of 1978, my brother, Dan Davis, along with his wife, Judy, and their four children were hired to act the parts of the Francis Cooke family at Plimoth Plantation in Massachusetts. Brochures about Plimoth Plantation describe the reconstructed Pilgrim village as a "living history" experience for visitors to enjoy, and in the process, to learn about the past by observing it in action. The plantation is a representation of life as it was in the year 1627, only seven years after the *Mayflower* landed at Cape Cod, Massachusetts.

To prepare for their roles as early settlers, it was necessary for the Davis family to become familiar with the Seventeenth Century English viewpoints on a variety of subjects—some of which could be distasteful to modern sensibilities. In all of their conversations they were required to express the then current attitudes of Englishmen. Modern concepts of equality, freedom, religious tolerance and respect for different cultures were unheard of in that era. Those early settlers were intolerant of foreigners, native Americans, Jews and even other Protestants who differed from their strict religious viewpoints. The Davises became familiar with the medical practices of the period and, more personally, took on the name and learned the life history of the particular settler each of them was portraying.

The Cooke family was from Scrooby, England, so Dan, Judy and the children learned to speak in that particular English dialect. The plantation's Shakespearean language expert had previously developed profiles for seventeen area dialects. As participants the Davises listened to audio-tapes, studied documents of the period and practiced speaking with other role players in order to become proficient in the dialect.

Judy and their daughter, Amy, learned how to do the typical female work of the colony. Examples of their tasks were grinding corn into flour, gardening, mending clothing by hand, tending the goats, cows and other animals and cooking meals on an open fireplace hearth. They concocted such delicacies as wild duck, bluefish, sweet cream custard, stewed eel and pottage. The latter is a thick soup of vegetables which sometimes included a little meat.

Dan and the boys, Chip, Fritz and Tim, occupied themselves with masculine jobs like, cutting, sawing and riving (splitting) timber, hoeing corn and other row crops in the nearby fields, using a musket for hunting, cleaning the stables of manure plus building and repairing structures employing the wattle and daub construction techniques. The daub (plaster-like material) was often mixed by foot in large wooden containers.

Because Dan and Judy's family members did not correspond exactly to the Francis Cooke family as it existed in 1627, a few minor adjustments in role assignments had to be made. In all, the Cooke family had seven children. John, the eldest son, came to North America on the *Mayflower* with his father in 1620. Jane, Elizabeth and Jacob arrived three years later with their mother, Hester, on the ship, *Anne*. Two of the seven, an unnamed girl, and Elizabeth were dead by the year 1627 and the two youngest, Hester and Mary, were not yet born. Therefore, Amy Davis, who was 17, played the role of 23 year old Jane Cooke, Chip Davis, who was 16, played the role of 20 year old John Cooke and Tim Davis, who was 11, played the role of Jacob Cooke, who was 9. That left Fritz Davis with no Cooke family member whose role he could assume. The problem was solved when he was assigned the part of John Morton, who was an indentured servant living with the Cooke family at that time. John and his family had arrived in North America in 1623 on the ship, *Anne*, along with Hester Cooke and three of the Cooke children.

One of my first questions to Dan and Judy when I heard that they had done the role playing at Plimoth Plantation all that summer was, "Did you <u>actually</u> <u>live</u> in the primitive houses at the plantation?" I had seen movies about Plimoth and was unthrilled at best about the residential accommodations provided. I must admit that I was relieved to learn that they had an apartment in the nearby city of Plymouth where they spent their off-duty hours and were able to go there for the night to sleep in present-day type beds as well as take baths or showers to maintain personal cleanliness.

Probably the most noteworthy thing about the Davises' role playing at the plantation during 1978 was an item of information learned a few years later. My mother did a large amount of genealogical research into the Davis Family. One of her contacts, a distant relative from Vermont, named Douglas Smith, proved that the Davises were actually related to Frances Cooke through a descendant of his eldest son, John Cooke. John had a grandson named Thomas Taber who was an ancestor of my great great great grandmother, Hannah (Taber) Davis. What a fortuitous coincidence! Dan and his family, unknown to them at the time, actually played the roles of their own ancestors at Plimoth Plantation that summer!

Judy (Rowe) Davis & Dan C. Davis
b. 1938          b. 1936

Children of
Dan & Judy Davis
(L to R) Tim, Chip (top), Fritz &
Amy

# CHAPTER 15

## *MAYFLOWER* CONNECTIONS AND ONE MISS

It seems as though every researcher who does much genealogical probing into his family's past always manages to discover a connection between his ancestors and the *Mayflower* passengers. Because nearly four hundred years have elapsed since that early three-masted ship landed in Cape Cod Bay in 1620, there probably are tens of thousands, if not millions, of descendants of those one hundred and two individuals in existence now.

Genealogists in the Davis family have managed to prove to their satisfaction that there exists a familial connection with three of the *Mayflower* passengers—

Francis Cooke, his son, John Cooke, and a third man named, George Soule.

Francis Cooke was born in England, probably in 1583. He was a member of William Brewster's religious sect, based in the city of Scrooby, which left England for Holland in the early 1600s. The members of the sect wished to practice their own type of Protestantism and found that impossible under the Stuart ruler, King James I. The group lived in Amsterdam for a few years and then moved to the university city of Leyden on the Meuse River about twenty miles distant. In Holland, Francis learned and practiced the trade of wool combing. He was married, probably in Amsterdam, to Hester le Mahieu. Records indicate that the couple had seven children altogether including Jane, John, Jacob, Elizabeth, Hester and Mary. Hester and Mary were born in America. One child, born in Holland and unnamed, died a short time after her birth.

When the sect (later called the Pilgrims) left Holland to establish a settlement in America, only Francis and his eldest son, John, made the initial crossing on the

*Mayflower*. His wife, Hester, and the other children followed three years later, in 1623 on the ship, *Anne*. Francis was one of the forty-one adult male signers of the Mayflower Compact. That compact was the agreement setting up the future government in the Plymouth Plantation and was the first instrument for self government in America.

Though about half of the 102 original settlers at Plymouth Plantation died during the first winter in America, Francis and John survived. They both lived to ripe old ages—Francis died in 1663 at the age of eighty and John died in 1695 at the age of eight-eight. The Davis connection to the Cooke Family is through one of John's grandsons, Thomas Taber. A descendant of Thomas was my great great great grandmother, Hannah (Taber) Davis, the wife of John E. Davis.

The third *Mayflower* passenger with ties to the Davis family was George Soule (sometimes spelled Georg Sowle). George was born in England sometime around the year 1600. He crossed the Atlantic as the servant of the

Edward and Elizabeth Winslow family. It is likely that he was indentured and worked for his passage by signing a contract of indenture with the Winslow family for a prescribed period of time. He, like Francis Cooke, also was a signer of the Mayflower Compact indicating that he was an adult—probably just twenty-one years old at the time.

George Soule married Mary Buckett in Plymouth and they had nine children: Zachariah, John, Nathaniel, George, Susanna, Mary, Elizabeth, Patience and Benjamin. Apparently George became well-to-do because at the time of his death in Duxbury, Massachusetts during the late 1670s, he owned properties in at least two different townships in addition to other holdings. He had been one of the colony's volunteers who fought against the Indians in the Pequot War of 1637. One of his sons, Benjamin Soule, was killed in 1676 during King Phillip's War between the colonists and the Wampanoag Indians.

I am uncertain as to exactly how the Soule family is related to the Davis family other than, like the Cooke family, it is through my great great great grandmother, Hannah Taber. The <u>real</u> genealogists in the family assure me it is a fact and that is good enough for me.

Much of the information for these stories I gleaned from the notes of my mother, Ernestine (Williamson) Davis, which she made while researching. Her efforts toward learning about the family were accomplished prior to the computer era. Therefore all of her information was obtained in a labor-intensive way—that is she wrote hundreds of letters to family members and other individuals, as well as various private and governmental agencies. I have found that the largest part of the data she obtained was accurate, but there are a few exceptions. One of those exceptions has to do with the *Mayflower*.

In one of Mother's notes she wrote about one of my great great great great great grandmothers, Deborah (Underhill) Wheeler. The note said, "She was a descendant of Captain John Underhill who came with Governor Winthrop on the *Mayflower* in 1630." I have no idea where she learned that tidbit of information because she gave no source for it. Two items in the note caught my attention: the date and the name Governor Winthrop. The *Mayflower* came to America in 1620, not 1630, and Winthrop was a governor of the Massachusetts Bay Colony, not Plymouth Plantation. 1630 <u>was</u> the year that the Massachusetts Bay Colony was established at Boston. I looked on the computer for a listing of the original settlers of that colony. Eureka! There I found the name, Captain John Underhill. So, instead of our ancestor being one of the *Mayflower* passengers, he was one of the original settlers of Massachusetts Bay Colony a mere ten years later. I felt pleased that Mother's research result was deficient in only one way—that of indicating that John Underhill was on the *Mayflower*. To my way of thinking, her efforts were fully vindicated.

# CHAPTER 16

## A MOHAWK INDIAN IN THE FAMILY

According to certain relatives who have done extensive family genealogical research, my great great great grandmother, Sarah (DeWitt) Rosencrants, was a full-blooded Mohawk Indian. I have seen little solid evidence to prove the authenticity of that statement but, on the other hand, have seen nothing that disproves it either. One fact that does give the story some small credence is that Sarah, her daughter Jane (my great great grandmother), her granddaughter, Olive, (my great grandmother) and her great granddaughter, Nettie (my grandmother) all share a common trait of very high cheekbones. That shared family characteristic gives each of them the traditional look of Native Americans but it does not prove anything.

The Mohawk Indians were native to what is now northern New York State. They were one of the early joiners of the Iroquois federation of tribes which later became the Iroquois Longhouse and eventually developed into the Six Nations Iroquois Federation. The federation subdued all the tribes from the St. Lawrence River on the north to Tennessee on the south and from Maine on the east to Michigan on the west.

Some historians claim that if the Six Nations had allied themselves with the French during the French and Indian Wars that the future United States likely would have become French. However, the Iroquois, under the leadership of Joseph Brant, a Mohawk chief, sided with the British instead. Chief Joseph later led the Iroquois forces fighting along side the British during the American Revolutionary War. After his victory, George Washington punished the Mohawks by burning their villages and forcing them to leave the New York State area and settle on reservations in Ontario, Canada.

I have often wondered how Sarah and her family came by the last name of DeWitt. Though I have no proof, I like to conjecture that they took on a French last name as a tribute to the ancestry of the residents of their adopted homeland in Ontario. Sarah was born near the end of the 1700s approximately twenty years after the end of the Revolutionary War. Somehow she met James Rosencrants of neighboring Michigan and they were married. One of Sarah and James's children, Jane, was born in 1825. Jane married Josiah Harvey Stephens and had a daughter, Olive, in 1854. Olive was wed to Stephen Johnson and their eldest child, Nettie, who was born in 1882, was destined to become my paternal grandmother.

Three of the photographs from my collection are purported to be likenesses of Sarah DeWitt and her daughter, Jane Rosencrants. Though I have no proof that information is correct, the photos do give rise to interesting study. Each of them contains objects likely of Indian derivation. Examples are the necklace and scarf pin worn by Jane in the single picture of her, plus the blankets worn as shawls by both Sarah and Jane in two of the photos.

When I carefully compared the unproven photos of Jane with the authenticated one in my collection, I found definite facial similarities. Though the two subjects are of different ages, in both of them the high cheekbones are obvious as well as the shape of the mouth and nose. In my judgment, the photographs depict the same person as a young lady and as an elderly lady. Once again I would like to emphasize that all of this is unproven, but it does help make the family story more interesting. Both history and family genealogy are fascinating subjects for scrutiny and study. I think it is intriguing that one of my female ancestors probably was a full-blooded Native American which would make my ethnic heritage the fraction one thirty-second Indian.

Jane (Rosencrants) Stephens
(1823 – 1883)
(authenticated)

Jane (Rosencrants) Stephens
(not authenticated)

Sarah (DeWitt) Rosencrants
(not authenticated)

Jane (Rosencrants) Stevens (left)
& Sarah (DeWitt) Rosencrants
(not authenticated)

# CHAPTER 17

## THE <u>ACTUAL</u> FIRST TUSCOLA COUNTY SETTLER

My great great grandparents, Ebenezer and Phebe (Burhans) Davis, usually are given credit for being the first permanent settlers in what was eventually to become Tuscola County. However, that tidbit of information is a little misleading when one examines the facts. Of course many generations of Native Americans had lived in the area for possibly hundreds of years before the first explorers or settlers of European heritage ever set foot there. Moreover, the Davises were not even the first non-Indians to move into that region either. A young man named Edwin Ellis deserves that credit. As it turns out he had a Davis connection as well.

Mr. Ellis, who was born in Vermont in 1811, drove a wagon pulled by a yoke of oxen across Ontario, Canada to Detroit in 1835. Ellis, like the Davises, had resided for a number of years in New York State. He, however, lived in Livingston County in the central western part of the state, whereas they lived first in Albany County, in the east, and later moved to the area near Niagara Falls in western New York. Ellis arrived in Tuscola County on November 24, 1835, over six months before Ebenezer brought his family to the area. The difference between Ellis's residency in the county and the Davises' is that they remained there whereas he left for a number of years before coming back again to become a permanent inhabitant.

Because he arrived in the Michigan wilderness late in the year, Mr. Ellis was unable to build a cabin for shelter, therefore he spent that first winter living in a tent on the bank of Perry Creek south of the present village of Tuscola. The six plus months before his first neighbors, the Davises, arrived apparently were rather lonely for him as he was a single man.    It is likely that Ellis was extremely gratified when Mr. and Mrs. Davis, with their eleven children, showed up in their covered wagon during the following June.

In 1837, Edwin moved to Saginaw, about twenty-five miles west of the Davis farm.  He remained there for two years before returning to Tuscola County and homesteading two miles north of the village of Tuscola. Apparently one of the things that drew Mr. Ellis back to Tuscola County was his interest in Cynthia Ann Davis, the eldest of Ebenezer and Phebe's daughters.   The young couple married in Tuscola in early1839 but Cynthia Ann's stay at her new home was to be very short.  She died that same year at the age of twenty-one.   I speculate that childbirth was the cause of her death because the records show that their daughter, Clarissa, was born in the latter part of that same year.   During that era of non-existent medical facilities and families with large numbers of children, giving birth always was a life threatening experience.

Recently, on a trip back to Michigan, I visited the Tuscola Cemetery where many of my Davis ancestors are buried. While looking around at the various grave sites, I came across one for the Edwin Ellis Family. There, among the grave markers, I located Cynthia Ann's stone.

After Cynthia Ann's death, Edwin remained a widower for four years. In 1844 he wed his second wife, Mary Hunter, who like Ellis, was born in Vermont. Her family had moved west from their state of origin and first settled in Ohio but eventually moved to the Township of Pine Run in Genesee County, Michigan. They had been there for nearly a decade prior to her marriage to Ellis.

Edwin and Mary lived together on the Ellis homestead in Tuscola County for nearly two decades. I'm uncertain how many offspring the couple had, but there was at least one daughter named Caroline. Ellis was a successful farmer and also active in township politics during those years. He passed away on May 27, 1881 at the age of seventy-one. His widow, Mary, continued to live on the homestead after her husband's death.

During the Tuscola Centennial celebration in 1935 a descendant of the Ellis family paid tribute to Edwin and noted the fact that he <u>was</u> the first settler. In addition, an article and a photograph appeared in the <u>Flint Journal</u> at the time. In the article, Ellis's oldest surviving granddaughter, Mrs. Lola O. Ormes who was a Flint resident, reminisced about her grandfather's arrival in the county. That was somewhat unusual because in most history books and articles about early Michigan, much note is taken of the Davises being the first <u>permanent</u> settlers of Tuscola County, and because of that, one is likely to overlook the fact that Edwin Ellis was the <u>actual</u> first settler in the county.

Mrs. Lola O. Ormes
(Granddaughter of Edwin Ellis)

# CHAPTER 18

## A LETTER FROM EBENEZER DAVIS

The following letter was written by my great great grandfather, Ebenezer I. Davis, in 1844. That was eight years after he and his wife, Phebe (Burhans), moved to the forested wilderness of Tuscola County, Michigan. Ebenezer and Phebe were born, grew up and married in the small town of Westerlo in Albany County, New York. They had five children while living there: James Hervey (my great grandfather), Cynthia Ann, Alonzo W., Amos and Alexander W.

About 1825, Ebenezer, Phebe and their children pulled up stakes in Albany County and moved west to Niagara County, New York. Davis family lore tells us that they lived near enough to Niagara Falls that one could hear the roar of the rushing water from their home. The Davises lived in that location for about ten years during which they had six additional children: Oliver Hunt, William Henry, Amy Jane, Stephen A., Sarah Grace and Martin Van Buren.

The year 1836 found the Davises once again on the move. They traveled west by covered wagon crossing Ontario, Canada and entering Michigan at Detroit. From there the family headed northwest through the wilds of eastern Michigan. In June of that year, they settled on a land grant along the Cass River in what is now the southwestern part of Tuscola County and lived there the balance of their lives. The last three of their fourteen children were born in that location. They were: Helen Amelia, who was the first white child born in the county, Eleanor M. and Hester Ann Elizabeth.

Ebenezer wrote this letter to his father, John E. Davis, who had remained behind and still lived in Westerlo, New

York. Hannah (Taber), Ebenezer's mother, died just a little over two years previous to his writing the letter.

My father, Dayton Davis, who was Ebenezer and Phebe's great grandson, told me that the original of the letter was brought back to Michigan by a Mr. Palmeter, whose mother was the daughter of Ebenezer's younger brother, Lewis. Therefore Mr. Palmeter would be Ebenezer's grand nephew. It is difficult for me to figure out why he carried the letter with him to the West, but I'm very pleased that he did. It is the only known writing of any consequence by Ebenezer Davis which has survived. I have attempted for years to locate the original, hand-written copy of the letter but have had no success. I added the words in brackets [ ] throughout the text of the letter.

*Tuscola, Mich.*
*April 26, 1844*
  *Kind Father,*

*I take this opportunity to write a few lines to you. I received your letter last summer and have been waiting for one thing and another to get ready to write to you.*

*You wrote to me of Mother's and Betsey's death. [Betsey was Ebenezer's younger sister.] I had heard of them by Ruth Allen's letter before. I meant to come and see you before this time as I hoped to see my mother again in this life, but it is otherwise ordered and there is a power that knows what is best and it is of no use for us to murmer or repine.*

*It seems that death has been very busy amongst you since I left you and it seems to me that I would be a stranger now in my native home knowing none of the new race nor they not knowing me. But I think of coming down to see you.*

*We thought we should get away this summer, but Phebe thinks it is doubtful whether she can leave the girls to keep house this summer  as most of the boys will be home most of the summer. But we mean  to come to you as soon as we can, this season if possible.*

*Alonzo [Their son who was twenty-three years old at the time] talks of going  to the state of New York this season but whether he will get to Westerlo or not, I don't know.*

*Hervey [My great grandfather, who was twenty-seven] is at home  and lives with us. He bought a piece of land last fall joining ours.*

*Amos [Their twenty-one year old son] is at home at present. The boys  have been making shingles this spring and will make until the first of June before they raft them down to Saginaw. Shingles fetch $1.25 a thousand at Saginaw and they can raft one hundred thousand at a time, more if they have them. It is only 20 miles by the river from our place to Saginaw and 16 by land.*

*Alexander [Their twenty year old son] has  gone out to work for the season. Oliver [Eighteen years old] and William [Sixteen years old] work at home with Hervey and me.*

*We have 12 acres of wheat sown and plant about 8 acres of corn this season besides oats, barley, potatoes and rutabagas. We have about 20 head of cattle, 6 head of poneys, 8 sheep and 10 hogs. We only got the sheep a year ago. That is the first that was fetched in the town. It was supposed the wolves would kill the sheep but they have never troubled ours yet. Oliver caught a wolf in a trap a few days ago.*

*Oliver is the greatest trapper and hunter amongst the boys. He has got a rifle that loads 100 balls to the pound and he kills as often as if the balls were as big again.*

*Amos killed two deer at one shot since we lived here with his rifle. There is plenty of game here in the woods such as elk, moose, bear, wolves, wildcats, fishers (or black cat), some wild turkeys and along the river, otter, mink, mushrats and plenty of coons. The political coons are about used up in this state. [I would like to know what he meant by that sentence.]*

*Since I wrote you we have built a barn 30 by 45 feet with a swing beam and 18 foot floor to thresh with ponies and we want to build a 70 foot shed this fall.*

*We made about 600 pounds of [maple] sugar this spring. It has been a forward spring. The 15<sup>th</sup> of this month the woods were green with feed for the cattle. The leeks and other wild flowers were up half leg high and cattle got a plenty to eat without foddering. We have every spring until last spring let our young cattle go by the first of April but last spring it was the 10<sup>th</sup> of April before the snow went off, but there was no frost in the ground so feed started immediately.*

*This is the greatest country for raising stock I ever saw. The winter light and plenty of feed in summer.*

*Chances to cut as much hay on the old fields cleared by the Indians and on the prairies as we are a mind to.*

*Our rivers are full of fish, the Rock and Black Bass, Pickerel, Pike, Catfish and Sturgeon. We spear our fish. We never have had a seine [net] yet. Our boys have speared 25 Sturgeon in one night.*

*This is as good a grain country as Lewiston [Where they lived for ten years near Niagara Falls] was, or better, as the land is dryer and equally as rich.*

*There is an Indian Reservation joining us of 8000 acres that the Government bought of the Indians. As* *handsome land as ever you saw. It is now $2.50 per acre and stands at that price until a year from next September. Then it comes down to $1.25 per acre that can be bought for State Scrip or Warrants which last you can get for 55 cents on the dollar which would make 80 acres cost $55. The timber is Maple, with some Beech, Elm, Basswood, White and Black Oak, Ironwood, Wild Plums, with "ridges of Pine" well watered with rivers and brooks. North of our river 5 ½ miles is a river the Indians call Cheboyganing that empties into the Saginaw River 8 miles below Saginaw. Five miles further north is the Quanacassee which empties into Saginaw Bay. The land on these rivers is as handsome as any in the world and between them as handsome and good land as any in western New York, but you must come out and see for yourselves.*

*I should think that Father and Darius [He was Ebenezer's 23 year old younger brother] could come out. You can come in about a week when you get started and traveling is cheap. You can get to Buffalo for about $5.00 and from there to Detroit for $2.50. Daniel Haines is here at present and is going to move here in the fall and some* *five or six families with him. They are tired of the openings and they want to get where they can make their own sugar and cut tame hay.*

*Daniel has learnt that his brother, Anthony, is somewhere in your town and he wants when you write to me to send him where he lives so he can write to him. If you see any that want to come out west, tell them to come here. If any country will suit them this will. The advantages of sending to market can't be beat. We can start from our house and go to Detroit by water and from there all over the world.*

*The greatest fisheries here winter or summer there is in the United States. Whitefish in summer and trout in winter. There were tons of trout carried from Saginaw last winter. Send as many Democrats as you can, although our County is Democratic our town is Whig by a small majority.*

*We have a new Tannery started here—the building is 30 by 64 Feet, a new grist mill, a saw mill, a frame school house, two blacksmiths, carpenters. I can't write half that I want to. You must some of you come out and see us and see for yourselves. I send to all of you, Father, Brothers and Sisters, give my respects to all of my friends, especially Oliver Hunt. Tell him that we are coming down soon as we can to make him a visit. Give my respects to Asa, Tish, Ruben and Deborah. [I don't know who Asa, Tish or Ruben were, but Deborah was Ebenezer's eldest sister who was 45 at the time.] Of course you will send this letter to all the boys that don't live in your neighborhood. Tell Samuel's wife [Samuel was one of Ebenezer's younger brothers who was 38 at the time.] she will Remember the children's names to Van Buren, and the younger ones are Helen, Eleanor, Hester Ann Eliza being the last one. We wanted to fill up as many names as we could. We have 13 children alive, the youngest being 2 ½ years old. [Cynthia Ann, the couple's eldest daughter died in 1840 at the age of twenty-one.]*

*Yours affectionally,*
*E. Davis*

*Phebe says I must give her respects to all of our friends and relations and especially Oliver Hunt. Tell him our Oliver is the tallest Davis yet, he is 6 foot high. You need not show this part of the letter to strangers. I send this to the boys. In the year 1840 I was elected Justice of the Peace, in 1842 I was elected Town Clerk and Assessor and Overseer of the Poor. The present year my term for Justice of the Peace expired, I was re-elected Justice of the Peace  and Town Clerk and I hold the highest office in the School District,  that is Moderator, but I have friends among the Whigs although  they know me to be a strong Democrat.*

Ebenezer I. Davis
(1797 – 1880)

Ebenezer Davis Trunk
(brought to Michigan from New
York State in 1836)

Westerlo, New York
Albany County

Westerlo, New York
Albany County

# CHAPTER 19

## THE DAVIS FERRY SERVICE

Ebenezer and Phebe (Burhans) Davis came across Canada from Niagara County in New York State and settled in the Lower Peninsula of Michigan during June of 1836. Their land grant homestead was situated a mile and a half west of the present village of Tuscola on the north shore of the Cass River. They built their house and farm buildings (none of which survive today) on a slight knoll overlooking a meandering un-named creek which flows in a generally southwest direction and empties into the Cass River on the south end of the property.

The Cass River provided one of the most important means of transportation for the early members of the

Davis Family. My father, Dayton W. Davis, who was Ebenezer and Phebe's great grandson, told me an intriguing story about the family's use of the Cass. Dad heard the tale as a part of the family lore passed down from his father, William E. Davis.

For years after the family settled on the property, the nearest bridge across the Cass River was ten miles downstream at Bridgeport, a few miles from Saginaw. Over the next few years, more and more settlers moved into the Tuscola area and occasionally it was necessary for them to cross the river. Some had small rowboats or canoes but not all. For those without any type of watercraft, crossing the river meant going twenty miles out of their way—ten miles to Bridgeport and ten miles back—a long trek on foot.

The Davis boys realized that they could seize upon that window of opportunity and earn some money while doing so. Several of Ebenezer's sons, including my great grandfather, James H. Davis and a couple of his brothers, started a small ferrying business on the river where it bordered the Davis farm. They used their rowboat to take people and light freight back and forth across the river and charged their passengers a small fee for each crossing. The money they received from the ferry service helped augment the income they received from making and then shipping wooden shingles to Saginaw to be sold there.

The Davis ferry service was taken over by younger siblings when the older boys married and moved away from the family farm. In all, there were eight sons in the family. The ferry business lasted for a number of years but eventually became redundant when a wooden bridge was built across the Cass River in the Village of Tuscola only a mile and a half to the east and the Davises were forced to find other means of earning a living..

After I retired from teaching, I became interested in studying our family roots. My father was a virtual font of information and stories about our ancestors and many of the things he told me whetted my curiosity for learning as much as I could about the family's past. Among the various stories Dad told me, was the one about the ferry service and I found it intriguing. He also pointed out exactly where the original Davis home had been situated on the property bordering the river. Having that information convinced me that further investigation would at least be interesting and might even shed further light on the history of the Davis family.

In 1994 I stopped at what had been Ebenezer's farm in order to see if I could find any remnants from the time that the Davis Family had lived there. The then current property owners showed me their Abstract of Title for the acreage which listed the ownership history of the farm. The document, which I was able to copy, indicated that Ebenezer and Phebe Davis bought the property from the government in 1836 and later it was passed down to various members of the family including my great grandfather, James H. Davis, and his siblings, Alonzo W. Davis, Martin Van Buren Davis, Amy Jane (Davis) Holmes, Amos Davis, Oliver H. Davis and William H. Davis. Eventually the property was sold out of the family.

After obtaining permission from the owners, I wandered up and down the rows of a bean field looking for artifacts. I was surprised to find literally hundreds of fragments of pottery and china lying in the area where the old house had stood. In addition to the pottery shards I found the remains of a pipe made from hardened clay that had been used for smoking tobacco. During my exploration I went down to the river and walked along the bank. As I did so I looked across the quietly running water and thought about my forbears who, about a hundred and fifty years ago, had ferried their passengers from one bank to the other, probably in that very spot. In that moment I felt a close connection to my past.

Five of Ebenezer & Phebe Davis's
Children
(L to R) Amos, Sarah Grace, James
Hervey, Amy Jane, Oliver Hunt

# CHAPTER 20

## THE WOOD CARVERS

My paternal grandfather was William Edward Davis. He was born near Tuscola, Michigan in 1864. His parents were James Hervey and Frances Marie (Weldon) Davis. William's first wife, Amelia Hustler, died giving birth to their second child. About a year later he married my grandmother, Nettie Johnson, who was an eighteen year old neighbor girl. He was thirty-six at the time and exactly twice the age of his bride.

William and Nettie, though they had six children together including my father, had a very rocky marriage. Several reasons for that state of affairs come to mind. One is that he was nearly a generation older than she. Their disparity in age and activity seemed to become even more apparent as the years passed. Another reason for their marriage's lack of success is that they had decidedly different types of personalities. William was the contemplative and intellectual type who was an avid reader, whereas Nettie was a no nonsense, hard working, practical person who did not believe in fancy frills such as education. She thought that individuals who spent time reading were merely lazy people.

In spite of their differences the couple managed to live together for a little over forty years. Finally, in 1942 my father, while visiting his parents, learned that their situation had come to a head. Nettie remained living in the house but William had moved out and had taken up residence in the miniscule sap shanty in the woods at the back of the farm. That was an 8 X 10 foot building with a large flat metal tray atop a wood-burning stove which was used for boiling maple sap into syrup. The shanty was totally unsuitable for human habitation. William and Nettie adamantly refused to reconcile their dispute so Dad gathered up a few of Grandfather's belongings and brought them and him back to our house to stay.

Grandfather Davis was a great story teller who seemed to have total recall of everything that had happened to him during the seventy-seven years that he had been on Earth. My siblings and I loved having him in our household because he was most entertaining, but that feeling was not shared by my mother. Adding him to the family meant more work for her and she was already burdened with caring for four children in a house that had no running water, no central heating and no bathroom.

One of the items that Grandfather brought with him when he came to live with us was a walking stick. It was no ordinary cane and it impressed me because it was not only beautiful but unusual as well. The cane was made from a reddish colored hard wood, like cherry or walnut and had a smooth round knob for a top. The length tapered down from the knob to the floor. What made the object so uncommon was that there was a deep but narrow groove in the wood that gracefully spiraled around and around the cane from one end to the other and gave it a distinctive serpentine appearance.

Previously I had seen the cane on a number of occasions but had never looked at it carefully. After moving in with us Grandfather often used it to help him get around the house and yard and that gave me the opportunity to examine it. What I saw piqued my curiosity so I questioned him about where he had obtained such an elegant accessory. He was quick to say that he had made it himself and then proceeded to relate in much detail how that came to be.

One spring while walking in the woods on his farm, Grandfather noticed a young, straight sapling near his path which had a wild grape vine just starting to climb up its small trunk. That gave him an idea. He decided to give Mother Nature a helping hand so that they, together, could create something beautiful.

Over the next couple of years Grandfather trained the grape vine to spiral around the tiny tree. As the tree became larger, its growth partially enveloped the climbing vine along its entire length. When the tree had reached the height of five to six feet, Grandfather cut it down, stripped the bark off and then carefully pulled the vine out of the groove that enclosed it. He cut the small trunk to the proper length for a cane. Then he carved the ball-shaped knob and attached it to the top. After he had smoothed and polished the entire object, the resulting walking stick was a true work of art. Grandfather was proud of his creation and enjoyed telling the story of how he had made it. Sadly his stories ended when he passed away in 1943 only a little over a year after he and Grandmother separated.

Grandfather Davis had come by his talent for wood carving legitimately. His own father, James Hervey Davis, too, was an artist in wood. Among the items he carved was a child's rattle. The toy was tubular and about eight inches long. What made it particularly unusual and difficult to carve was that at each end there was a narrow cage enclosing a small ball which moved freely. The movement of the two balls made the rattling sound for children to enjoy. The balls could not have been added after the carving was done because the spaces between the bars of the cages were too narrow. Therefore they had to have been carved inside the cages from the same piece of wood. Great Grandfather Davis must have carefully inserted his knife between the bars to form the round balls. When the rattle was finished he painted it several different colors. However, during the one hundred and fifty years since then most of the pigments have faded.

James Hervey and his son William Edward Davis handed their wood carving talent down to the next generation as well. My father, Dayton Davis, after he retired, spent many hours carving canoe paddles for his own use as well as for other family members. I recall watching him use the sharp edge of a piece of broken glass to do some of the final smoothing of the paddles' curved surfaces. Some of those canoe paddles may still exist in the family. During that same period of time Dad also carved a number of axe handles which he used as replacements on both his single and double edged axes.

Grandfather's cane and Great Grandfather's toy rattle resided with various members of my family until they ended up in my possession. In 2005 I loaned both of the items to the Vassar Historical Society Museum. They were placed on display there as artifacts created by Tuscola County residents.

 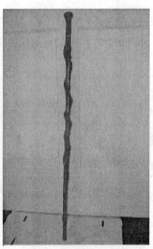

William E. Davis
(1864 – 1943)

Walking Stick
Carved by
William E. Davis

James Hervey Davis
(1817 – 1888)

Dayton W. Davis
(1907 – 2002)

Child's Toy Rattle
Carved by
James Hervey Davis

Canoe Paddles
Carved by
Dayton W. Davis

# CHAPTER 21

## A DAVIS JOINS THE GOLD RUSH

According to my research, the only relative on my father's side of the family who participated in the California Gold Rush of the late 1840s was my great grandfather's younger brother, Alexander W. Davis. He was no stranger to firsts in the Davis Family as he was the first to attend college and the only family member to become a legislator for the State of Michigan.

Alexander was born in Westerlo, Albany County, New York State on October 30, 1824. He was the fifth child of my great great grandparents, Ebenezer and Phebe Davis. When Alexander was a little over a year old the family moved to western New York State and settled near

Niagara Falls for a period of about ten years. Then in 1836 the Davises transplanted to Michigan. By that time there were eleven children in the family and Alexander was twelve years old.

While Alexander was a teenager, Ebenezer and Phebe's family established itself in what later was to become Tuscola County. Originally they purchased fifty acres along the Cass River from the Federal Government for $1.25 per acre. Their first dwelling was a log cabin, winter-proofed with tree bark, which sat on a small rise overlooking a creek flowing into the Cass. Over the next ten years the Davises added to their property, cleared the forest trees from the site, built a complete set of farm buildings and raised a variety of farm animals and crops.

Along with his brothers and sisters, Alexander attended school in the nearby Village of Tuscola. Later, according to a biographical sketch which I found in the Vassar Library, he attended Albion Seminary for a short period of time. The seminary was established in 1835 and later became Albion College. While at Albion, Alexander was a college classmate of Edwin B. Winans, who went on to become the twenty-second governor of the State of Michigan and served in that office from 1891 to 1892.

In 1843, when Alexander was nineteen, he left Tuscola County and went to work in Genesee County for $10.00 a month. One of the people who employed him as a farm laborer during the next few years was Judge Jeremiah R. Smith. Years later Alexander purchased the Judge's farm and he and his wife lived there during the latter part of his life.

The Mexican-American War began in the spring of 1846 and about a year later Alexander enlisted in Company A of the Fifteenth Michigan Infantry. He was part of General Winfield Scott's army of 9,000 troops that landed at the Gulf of Mexico port of Veracruz and fought its way westward toward Mexico City. Alexander participated in the victorious Battles of Churubusco and Contreras just south of the capital city. He was wounded in the right leg and was sent to a military hospital in Baton Rouge, Louisiana. Eventually Alexander was discharged from the army and returned to Michigan.

Apparently the war whetted Alexander's appetite for travel because in 1850 he once again left Michigan. The Gold Rush had begun at Sutter's Mill in California just over a year previous to that and he decided to try making his fortune there. Alexander took a circuitous but logical route to the West by traveling to New York City where he caught a boat to the Isthmus of Panama in the Gulf of Mexico. There, like the other would-be prospectors, he made his way across to the Pacific Ocean by boat, on foot and by mule back. (The first railroad across the Isthmus wasn't completed until five years after he made the crossing.) Upon reaching the Pacific, Alexander then boarded a ship for San Francisco. Over the next three years he mined for gold in the Sacramento Valley and, unlike thousands of others, found it a successful venture.

When Alexander was satisfied with the size of his new-found fortune, he took the same roundabout return route to Michigan from California. He settled in Grand Blanc Township of Genesee County and purchased Judge Smith's three hundred and sixty acre farm where previously he had worked as a paid laborer. In 1853 he married Harriet

McFarlen, daughter of Grand Blanc pioneer settler, Joseph McFarlen. The couple lived in a large, well appointed Center Street home on a portion of their farm bordering the southern edge of the Village of Grand Blanc. Their house faced the foot of Davis Street which was named in Alexander's honor. When Alexander and Harriet had been married for thirteen years they were blessed with the birth of a son, Joseph, on September 10, 1866. Sadly, however, Joseph lived for less than two months and passed away on November 8th of that same year.

Besides managing his farm over the following decades, Alexander also became active in local politics. He fulfilled the position of Township Treasurer, served as Justice of the Peace for a quarter century and became a member of the Genesee Bar. Alexander was instrumental in promoting the extension of the first railroad (The Flint and Holly Railroad Company) into Grand Blanc in 1864. He was one of ten local investors, along with his brother-in-law, John McFarlen, who put up a bond for the new enterprise. The railroad ran through the Davis farm property just west of his residence. About thirty years later, when the original two-story, brick Grand Blanc school building became unsafe for further use, Alexander was chosen as one of the three building committee members who were responsible for replacing the structure in 1890. He also subdivided a portion of his acreage which abutted Grand Blanc and the subdivision was called The A. W. Davis Addition.

At the time of the Civil War (1861 – 1865) Alexander widened his political horizons by serving two terms in the Michigan State Legislature. He was elected as an anti-slavery Republican and, while a member of that political body, became chairman of the Military Committee.

The Honorable Alexander W. Davis led an active, adventurous and full life and passed away on the first of April in 1899 slightly less than a year prior to his wife's passing. He was seventy-four and a half years of age at the time and though he and Harriet had no children who survived them, he left a noteworthy agricultural and political legacy for his adopted hometown.

Alexander W. Davis Home
Grand Blanc, Michigan

Grave of Alexander W. Davis
McFarlen Cemetery
(Grand Blanc Township)

# CHAPTER 22

## THE SAGA OF AMY JANE DAVIS

My great great grandparents, Ebenezer and Phebe Davis, had fourteen offspring over a period of twenty-four years. The children were born in three different locations—the first five in Albany County, New York, the next six in Niagara County, New York and the final three in Tuscola County, Michigan. My great grandfather, James Hervey, was the eldest of the fourteen siblings. Amy Jane, who was born on the Fourth of July in 1830, was among the six children from the Davis's Niagara County sojourn.

Amy Jane Davis was just a month short of six years of age when the Davis Family arrived in Michigan in June of 1836. When she was fifteen she married twenty-one year old Theodore F. Smith who lived between Birch Run and Bridgeport (about ten miles southwest of her parents' homestead). The couple lived on their farm there and eventually had four daughters. They were Erma Augusta, Anna Elizabeth, Elnora Cynthia and Alice Gladys. At the time their youngest daughter, Alice, was born in 1857, Theodore was serving as the Birch Run Township Supervisor for a one year term.

Theodore Smith entered the army as a lieutenant during the early part of the Civil War in 1861 and reported for duty with the Fifth Michigan Cavalry. Amy Jane was left at home with the daunting task of running the family farm in addition to caring for their four daughters. Her burden was exacerbated when Theodore failed to return to Michigan after hostilities ended in 1865. The family eventually learned that he went to Cairo, Illinois, married again and raised a second family. Years later, after Theodore had passed away, one of his sons from that second family visited Amy Jane in Flint where she was living with her daughter.

Amy Jane filed for divorce from Theodore, apparently using desertion as the grounds. After a divorce decree was granted she married the Hon. Alfred H. Holmes, originally from Saratoga, New York, who was twenty-five years her senior. According to <u>The History of Tuscola & Bay Counties</u>, Mr. Holmes is credited with building the first grist mill in Tuscola County. He erected it on Perry Creek south of the Village of Tuscola about 1841. Family lore tells us that the title, Hon., came about because Alfred had been a local judge or Justice of the Peace. At the time of their marriage, Mr. Holmes was a well-to-do Bridgeport farmer and, though he never adopted Amy Jane's daughters, he was a good father to them. That is evidenced by the fact that her third daughter, Elnora Cynthia, named her eldest son, Alfred Holmes Beech, after him.

Four years into their marriage, Amy Jane and Alfred Holmes had their only child, Edith. The Holmes family lived on the Bridgeport farm until Alfred's death in June of 1885, three months after his eightieth birthday. In spite of the quarter century disparity in age between the two, theirs was a happy and fulfilling marriage that lasted nearly twenty years.

Amy Jane Holmes outlived her husband by almost thirty-five years and lived well into the Twentieth Century. She spent those years among her children and grandchildren. At various times she resided with her daughter, Edith (Holmes) Chase in Flint, with another daughter, Elnora (Smith) Beech in Saginaw, with her granddaughter, Euseba (Davis) Becker of Mt. Morris and with her nephew, Howard Davis (son of her brother, Martin Van Buren Davis), in Tuscola. She even made several trips to Seattle, Washington to visit her second daughter, Anna (Smith) Finch, who lived there with her family all her married life.

Amy Jane (Davis) Smith Holmes's long life encompassed the early settlement of Michigan, the Mexican-American War, the expansion of the United States to the Southwest, the Civil War, the building of the first Transcontinental Railroad, the Spanish- American War and the United States involvement in World War I in

Europe. She passed away at her granddaughter's home in Mt. Morris, Michigan on April 26, 1920, only three months before her ninetieth birthday.

Amy Jane (Davis) Smith, Holmes
(1830 – 1920)

# CHAPTER 23

## THE TUSCOLA CENTENNIAL

The tiny Village of Tuscola hosted the Tuscola County centennial celebration in 1935. The townspeople and officials organized two days of activities in early July celebrating the hundredth anniversary of the arrival of the first settler. A large number of local residents, including some of my family members, took part in the presentations which drew crowds of visitors to the area. Because I was only three years old at the time, I have no personal memories of what transpired during those summer days, however, I managed to locate one of the Official Souvenir Programs, and additional information was passed down through the family. Those two sources form the basis for this vignette.

The centennial gala was held on Wednesday, July 3 and Thursday, July 4th. The festivities included athletic events, such as baseball games and a tug of war between the residents of various communities in the county, addresses by state and local government officials and band concerts as well as the presentation of an original play and pageant. There were a number of food stands and other attractions set up in the center part of the village in the triangle of the village school yard and many of the activities took place there. Just east of the general store there was an open-air dance floor. In addition, free showings of black and white movies were projected against the north wall of the I.O.O.F. Hall immediately across from the east end of the school yard.

Wednesday, the first day of the celebration, was designated as homecoming day. After a short band concert in the afternoon, the assembled group was treated to an address by the auditor general of the State of Michigan, John J. O'Hara. Next came the crowning of Mr. and Mrs. Delroy Palmer, as the Centennial King and Queen. They were the oldest couple in the county, and Mrs. Palmer, who was ninety-two years old, was the daughter of Lovira Hart, who, along with my great great grandparents, was one of the first settlers of the county. Mr. Palmer, born in Tuscola, worked in the lumber business for a period of time, then took up farming a mile north of the village and finally owned and operated a grocery and hardware store in Tuscola for twenty years prior to his retirement.

My grandfather, William Edward Davis gave a formal speech following the coronation ceremony. Grandfather Davis was a farmer who, with his family, lived a little over a mile south of the Village of Tuscola. He prided himself on being a scholar and a voracious reader of local, state and national history and, in addition, knowledgeable about the politics of the day. The centennial committee prevailed upon him to give a lecture on Tuscola's early settlement and the history of the Davis family. It was thought that he was well qualified for such a task considering he was the grandson of the first permanent settlers, Ebenezer and Phebe Davis, and someone very familiar with the local history. Additional historical sketches were presented by other dignitaries later in the program.

Wednesday evening at 8:30 the visitors enjoyed a presentation of the Tuscola County centennial play and pageant, called "The Homecoming." That segment of the festivities took place at the school yard in the middle of the Village, and was produced by a professional Jackson, Michigan dramatics company. Most of the many acting roles were performed by local citizens.

Thursday, the Fourth of July, was the second day of the centennial gala. In the morning there were individual athletic events and a second musical extravaganza presented by the Vassar High School concert band. Following the music there was yet another tug-of-war, this time involving the winner of the previous Vassar-Millington contest and a Frankenmuth team. Later the audience enjoyed an informal talk by Mrs. Lola Ormes of Flint, Michigan. Mrs. Ormes was the great granddaughter of Edwin Ellis who was the actual first settler in the county.

The centennial parade also was held that afternoon and it included over fifty colorful floats. The participants formed themselves at the western end of the village and, led by the Vassar High Band, marched the length of the main street to a temporary stage on the east side of town. There the parade dispersed and the crowd was treated to a talk by Louis C. Cramton, judge of the 40th Judicial Circuit Court.

A costumed re-enactment of the initial arrival in Tuscola County of Ebenezer and Phebe Davis (with their eleven children) in the 1830s was presented in the form of an historical tableau—something that was very popular during the early part of the Twentieth Century. Once again, local townspeople were selected to play various roles as members of the original Davis family.

Following the tableau, fireworks and a free movie projected on the north side of the IOOF Hall brought the exciting two-day celebration to an end.

I noted several things of particular interest about the photo of the Davis Family re-enactment which I found in my parent's picture collection. First is the exceedingly large number of Davis descendants who played roles in the pageant. Russell Davis and his wife, Ilda, acted the roles of Ebenezer and Phebe Davis. Their daughters, Marjorie, Marian and Geraldine all played parts as well as their son, Howard. Howard, in fact, only five years old at the time, played the role of the youngest of Ebenezer and Phebe's daughters, Sarah Grace Davis. Russell Davis and his children were direct descendants through Ebenezer and Phebe Davis's son, Martin Van Buren Davis. Another participant in the pageant, Harry Davis, was directly descended (as I am) from James Hervey Davis, Ebenezer's eldest son.

There were even two more of my cousins in the re-enactment. They were from my mother's side of the family and unrelated to the Ebenezer Davis family. The two were Betty and Don Baldwin, children of my mother's older sister, Florence, and her husband, Howard

Baldwin. The three of them, Betty, Don and their father, were born and grew up in Tuscola.

The last item about the photo that piqued my interest is that finally, after much study, I was able to figure out where it was taken. At first I thought that the dark, framed area in the background was a window, but then realized that it was a school chalkboard. The picture was taken in the two-room Tuscola School. The wood-slatted piece of furniture on which some of the actors are seated is what we, when I attended the school, called the "recitation bench." It stood next to the teacher's desk at the front of the classroom. For the purpose of taking the photograph, the bench had been moved from its usual location. It normally faced the chalkboard rather than presenting its back to it as shown in the picture.

History is a fascinating study and one can learn much about the story of the past through close examination of such artifacts as documents, drawings, newspaper articles and photos in addition to oral histories. I feel that a person's life is enriched by knowing as much as possible about his or her roots. The Tuscola Centennial celebration in 1935 gave me the opportunity to examine and learn additional information concerning one more small part of my family heritage.

Re-enactment of the Ebenezer
Davis Family
(1935)

Mr. & Mrs. Delroy Palmer
(Centennial King & Queen)

# CHAPTER 24

## THE BORN TEACHER

"Miss Davis" as she was known to all of us, was a school teacher for nearly two-thirds of her short life. In total she taught for thirty-four years and during that time affected the lives of hundreds of pupils, many of whom were her relatives. My own introduction to the world of classes, school and education in general, was under Miss Davis's watchful eye. She was my teacher from kindergarten through the first half of the second grade which was when she passed away. Years previous to that, during her tenure as a teacher at the Pinkerton School, another of her students was her own younger brother, Russell Davis. In addition, from kindergarten through the fifth grade, she taught my cousin, Harry Davis, as well as my older brother, Laurel.

Bessie Ruth Davis, to whom I was a second cousin once removed, was born on May 24, 1886 in her parents' farm home on Ormes Road, about a mile east of the village of Tuscola. She was the second child of Howard and Carrie (Veeder) Davis. Bessie was the only daughter in the family. She had a brother, John, who was a bit more than a year older than she, and a younger brother, Russell, who was nearly eleven years her junior.

After Bessie graduated from the tenth grade at the Tuscola School, she may have attended a semester or two of teacher instruction at the Tuscola County Normal School in Caro. (A couple of her relatives have varying memories about that bit of information.) Regardless of whether or not that was the case, Bessie began her teaching career in 1904 at the tender age of eighteen. The Pinkerton School was Bessie's first teaching assignment. It was a one room rural school about a mile east of the Davis farm on Ormes Road. Bessie taught all subjects in each of the grades, kindergarten through the eighth—a daunting task for any teacher but seemingly insurmountable for an eighteen year old girl just out of school.

Though she probably never completed a college degree, Bessie attended summer sessions and earned credits at several Michigan colleges, including Eastern Michigan in Ypsilanti and Central Michigan in Mt. Pleasant. I can sympathize with her being required to do that because I earned my master's degree from Central Michigan in the same way. On weekends during the school year and daily during the summers, I could be found trekking from Saginaw, where I lived, to Mt. Pleasant for class work, research and study. Unlike Bessie's, my traveling back and forth ended after a couple of years when I had completed the requirements for my degree, but hers continued for most of her teaching career.

Bessie believed in broadening her horizons by traveling and, at various times with local friends, took trips to such places as Grand Canyon National Park in

Arizona, Yellowstone National Park in Wyoming, Niagara Falls, and Watkins Glen on Lake Seneca in New York State. Bessie even invited one of her nieces, Marjorie (Davis) Squire, to accompany her on one of the trips. She also subscribed to the National Geographic Magazine and brought its issues to the Tuscola School. When I was a pupil there, those magazines, which she kept on a library shelf, provided me with my first real window on the rest of the world. I spend many happy hours poring over the colorful pages and absorbing information on places I dreamed of visiting some day. Happily, I can now say that many of those dreams did come true.

As mentioned above, Bessie's brother, seven year old Russell, was one of her first pupils at the Pinkerton School. Recently, Russell's daughter, Marian (Davis) Kosha, told me that it was common knowledge in the Davis family that if Russell misbehaved in school and was punished by Bessie, he received a double dose of punishment later on at home. Likely the poor boy chafed under such injustice and complained bitterly about the misfortune of having his older sister for a teacher.

Following her stay at the Pinkerton School, Miss Davis taught at various other one-room schools in the Tuscola area for the next twenty-five years. They included stints at the Hub School, the Whitney School and the Diamond School. In 1929 she accepted a position at the Tuscola Village School. The next nine years of Bessie's life were spent as the teacher in what we used to call the "little" room at the white, two-room school in the heart of the village. The term "little" did not refer to the size of the room, but instead had to do with the size and age of the pupils taught there. The primary room contained the kindergarten through the fifth grade. When pupils had passed the fifth grade they graduated to the "big" room where grades six through ten were taught. I remember only two of the teachers from that room—Mr. Jacoby and Mr. Taylor.

Bessie Davis remained single all her life. Her niece, Marjorie, did admit to me that the family sometimes speculated about Bessie and one eligible bachelor in Tuscola, however his name will not be revealed here. Marjorie said that the talk was likely just idle gossip anyway because she didn't believe that the couple ever went so far as to even have a date with one another. To those of us who knew her, Miss Davis was the proverbial "spinster school marm" who was married to her teaching job. A short time after she began teaching at the Tuscola School, she bought a large, two story home about a block from the school. She invited her parents, Howard and Carrie Davis, to live with her. By then they were retired and had turned their farm over to their son, Russell.

Miss Davis made an indelible impression on me during the three years I knew her. I recall she was kind, extremely intelligent and knowledgeable, plus she took her responsibilities seriously. As a teacher she was strict but fair. A number of the pupils, especially boys, were taller than she, but that made no difference because only Miss Davis was in charge in her classroom. She maintained a no-nonsense and business-like aura and I don't remember there ever being any serious disruptions. The fact that some of us were Miss Davis's relatives also carried no weight with her. We were treated exactly the same as all the other pupils. In case we broke the rules, we were punished and if we accomplished something exceptional, we were lauded.

A few weeks before we were to be let out of school for the Christmas vacation in 1938, Miss Davis came down with a serious case of pneumonia. She was treated at home for a short time but later her condition worsened and she was transferred to the Saginaw General Hospital about twenty miles west of Tuscola. There Miss Davis lapsed into a coma from which she never recovered. She passed away two days before Christmas at the age of fifty-two. Miss Davis was the first in her immediate family to die, so she was survived by her parents and her two brothers.

From reading her obituary in the <u>Flint Journal</u>, I learned more about Miss Davis's funeral. The service was held at the Atkins Funeral Home in Vassar On December 26, the day after Christmas. She was interred at the Davis plot in the Tuscola Cemetery on the high bank overlooking the Cass River. As an indication of the esteem in which she was held, Miss Davis's list of pallbearers read like a <u>Who's Who</u> of well-known men in the village of Tuscola. Following the service in Vassar a large crowd of relatives, friends, acquaintances, colleagues and former students gathered at the graveside to bid goodbye to "The Born Teacher."

Bessie Davis
& her Tuscola School
Pupils

Bessie Davis
(1886 – 1938)

Bessie Davis
& her Tuscola School
"Little Room" Pupils

# CHAPTER 25

## FOLLOWING UNCLE MICKEY'S FOOTSTEPS

Though he was the youngest in a family of eight children, my father's brother, Melvin Davis, died long before any of his older siblings. He was the only one who never reached the age of thirty years. Circumstances in his biography caused him to be the widest traveled member of the family up to the time of his death. Here is the story of Melvin's interesting but abbreviated life.

"Mickey," as he was known by everyone in the Davis clan, was born on February 17, 1917. That was just a little less than two months before the United States declared war on Germany and thus officially joined the Allies in their fight against the Central Powers during World War I.

Mickey's parents, especially his father, were rather "on in years" to be having a new baby. His mother, Nettie (Johnson) Davis, was thirty-five at the time and William Edward Davis was eighteen years her senior at fifty-three. Nettie ran a busy farm household and consequently much of the care for the new baby fell within the responsibility of his older sisters, Norma who was eight, Leona who was fifteen, and his half-sister, Ethel who was eighteen at the time.

The Davises lived on an eighty acre farm about a mile and a half south of the Village of Tuscola in the southwest corner of Tuscola County. They raised a few row crops on their sandy soil, as well as grain, corn and alfalfa to be used as feed for a small dairy herd. The family sold most of the milk from the cows as a cash crop. The rest they either drank themselves or used in the form of cream or butter. I recall asking Grandmother Davis if I could turn the crank on the cream separator in the basement of the farmhouse. The farm enterprise was nearly self-sufficient in that it also provided the Davises with beef from the cattle, pork from the hogs, meat and eggs from the small flock of chickens, sugar and syrup from a maple grove, fresh fruit from the orchard and vegetables from a garden plot.

Like his older brothers and sisters, Mickey learned to take on some of the farm responsibilities at a young age. Long before he was ten years old he already was familiar with the care and feeding of the chickens and other chores around the family enterprise. Because there was much work to be done on a farm in that era and moreover since his parents were strict taskmasters, Mickey and his siblings had little free time available for their own personal interests.

From the age of five, Mickey walked to the nearby Hub School along with the neighbor children and other family members. Each year from September through May, they took instructions in the one room school from the current school teacher there. I have several photos which show the teacher and pupils posing in front of the school. The pictures indicate that usually there were less than ten pupils in total for all of the grades, kindergarten through the eighth. When he was graduated from the eighth grade at the Hub School, Mickey transferred to the two-room school in the village of Tuscola. There he completed his education through the tenth grade by about the year 1933 or 1934.

With his formal education behind him, seventeen year old Mickey chose to stay on his parents' farm and help them manage it. By that time, his father, William, was in his late sixties and unable to do the necessary heavy labor by himself. All of Mickey's older siblings, including my father, had left the farm, married and were earning their livelihoods elsewhere.

Though most of the family had dispersed, the Davis farm continued to be the common meeting point for all of them. I recall attending many impromptu gatherings in the large white house shaded by a giant maple tree. Grandfather Davis had transplanted that tree from the woodlot at the back of the farm when it was a small sapling. Often the clan converged around the oval-shaped, expandable table in the large kitchen in order to partake of one of Grandmother Davis's sumptuous dinners.

Those meals usually turned out to be noisy affairs where the politics of the day were often the main topic of conversation. The Davises were a well-read family and everyone had strong opinions with no hesitancy about expressing their opinions. The older family members generally supported the Democrats in the government and conversely, the younger ones, Mickey included, favored Republican points of view. Frequently the discussions turned into shouting matches which, if there had been close neighbors, easily would have been overheard. As it happens the nearest farmhouse was about a quarter of a mile down the road and well out of earshot.

Another favorite topic of conversation was religion. I don't remember any of the family attending church regularly, but all of them had read the Bible and each interpreted its stories differently. No subject was off limits, thus all members of the group stated their thoughts openly. Because all of the fifteen to twenty people around the table usually resorted to shouting in order to have their views heard, often the result was a cacophonous melee. I came away from the discussions with the feeling that the Davises never thought of religion as being an emotional or deeply personal subject, but instead that it was more of an intellectual exercise to be enjoyed by everyone.

Mickey had a very light complexion which easily turned red at the slightest embarrassment, to the delight of the rest of the family. He was never able to shed the title "baby of the family," so his older siblings often amused themselves by teasing him unmercifully. Frequently he also was the butt of jokes and harmless, though embarrassing family pranks. Mickey accepted all of the harassment with good grace and, because he was intelligent and had a well-developed sense of humor himself, he managed to respond in kind.

Uncle Mickey was the only one of the Davis children to remain on the home farm so, as an added financial incentive for him and to encourage him to stay, his name was added to the deed, making him half owner in the enterprise along with his parents. That arrangement seemed to work out well for him as well as the elder Davises, at least for a time. Just under a decade later, however, the world political situation intervened. Four days after the December, 1941 Japanese attack on Pearl Harbor in the Hawaiian Islands, the United States government declared war on the Axis Powers, thereby officially entering World War II.

Almost immediately after the declaration, patriotic excitement swept the nation. It was spurred on of course by a well-planned and vigorous propaganda blitz from the federal government. Mickey, along with thousands of other young Americans, was caught up in the impassioned fervor and was eager to defend his country. He joined the navy and entered basic training at the Great Lakes Naval Training Center in Illinois. That was the beginning of his travels—he had never before been out of the state of Michigan. The center was forty miles north of Chicago on Lake Michigan. He was one of over a million sailors trained at that site during World War II.

After graduating from basic training, Mickey was sent to a naval center in Virginia for advanced instruction. While attending mechanics school there, he and his naval buddies became familiar with that area of the country by spending their weekend leaves traveling. Among their favorite destinations was nearby Richmond, the capital of Virginia. On one of those excursions, Mickey was introduced to a young Richmond lady named Irene Thomas. The two found that they had much in common as they both embarrassed easily and were rather shy in public. Irene and Mickey began dating, fell in love and were married within a year from the time they first met one another.

The marriage was rather a sporadic one because Mickey's naval duties required his presence aboard ship a large percentage of the time. However, he did manage to get one long leave, just before he was sent to England to join the action there. During that leave Mickey brought his bride to Michigan to meet the family for the first time. The year was 1944; I was eleven years old and recall the visit rather vaguely. I do remember distinctly, however that the entire Davis clan was thoroughly intrigued with Irene's delightful Southern accent. (We called it her "Southern Drawl.") She became an immediate family favorite and Mickey showed her off with obvious pride. They made a handsome couple and seemed ideally suited to one another.

Uncle Mickey's leave in Michigan was soon over and the couple returned to Richmond where Irene was going to live while he was away in Europe. She held a wartime job there and that was where her relatives lived. In the early spring Mickey's naval squadron was sent to England to be a part of the joint Allied training exercises preparing for the D-Day invasion of German-occupied France across the English Channel.

The term "D-Day" is military jargon designating a secret date on which a particular war operation is to begin. Uncle Mickey took part in the most famous of all the D-Days when his LST (Landing Ship Tank) was among the nearly 9,000 total ships that crossed the English Channel on June 6, 1944. The ship was assigned the mission of dropping military personnel and tanks on the French Coast in the Province of Normandy. The invading Allied ground troops then attacked the German-built defensive wall and after deadly hand-to-hand fighting, managed to break through the perimeter. That success, however, had a large price attached to it. The cost in human life was enormous.

Uncle Mickey was one of those casualties. His ship was blown up in the waters off the coast of Normandy and all hands were lost at sea. We aren't certain on which exact date that occurred, but the telegram sent to the family said he was officially listed as "missing in action" on June 19, 1944. Much later I learned that the government uses a formula for determining the official death dates of service personnel whose bodies are never recovered. That date is one year and one day after the serviceman was listed as missing. Therefore, Mickey's official death date would be June 20, 1945.

Mickey's wife, Irene, and all of the other members of the Davis Clan were devastated by his death at such a young age. He had shown great promise for the continuation of the family farm and name. Everyone had assumed that he would have children to carry on the family name and they would be instrumental in keeping the family farm intact. But such was not to be the case.

After Mickey's death, Irene, as his widow and principal heir, automatically became co-owner along with his mother, Nettie Davis, of the Davis Farm in Tuscola County. His father, William, had died the previous year, in 1943. That state of affairs lasted until a few years after World War II ended in 1945. During that time Irene came to realize that she had little desire to maintain half interest in a farm in Michigan, hundreds of miles from her own home in Virginia. Consequently she contacted her former mother-in-law and asked if the family had any interest in buying her out. Nettie, who had some money put by in savings, discussed the matter with other members of the family. Eventually she made a cash offer which Irene accepted. In a short time Irene, accompanied by her sister, "Red," visited Michigan for the second and last time in order to sign the transfer of ownership papers for the Davis farm.

From there we don't take up the story again until the year 2001, about fifty years later. By that time I had retired from teaching school in Michigan and had moved to Albuquerque, New Mexico in order to take advantage of the mild Southwestern climate. In late August of that year a couple of Albuquerque friends and I went on a holiday trip to France. We flew into the Charles De Gaulle International Airport near Paris and then used a rental auto to travel to the province of Brittany where we had rented a home near the city of St. Lo. We planned to use that home as our base for making a number of side trips to various sites in northern France.

The side trip that I was most eager to take was a visit to the Normandy coast and to walk in the footsteps of the invading Allied forces from D-Day, 1944. Near the end of our stay in France I drove the fifty miles or so to Utah and Omaha Beaches where the invasion occurred. On a bright and breezy day, I walked the white sand beaches and looked out at the dark blue waters of the English Channel. I thought about Uncle Mickey and his navy companions who lost their lives delivering the men and materials for the fateful invasion.

Further up the Normandy coast I visited the American Cemetery and United States War Memorial near the village of Colleville-sur-Mer. I was deeply moved by that lovely tribute to the thousands of fallen servicemen who had given their lives for the Allied cause. At the memorial itself which was a many-columned circular monument I located Uncle Mickey's name on the Wall of the Missing. Though there are over fifteen hundred names inscribed on that curved surface, I had little problem locating the one I had come to view. I choked up and shed a tear or two when I saw "MELVIN L. DAVIS" carved into the salmon-colored marble of the perimeter wall. I was pleased and proud to be related to the man who was honored in that eloquent way.

## POSTSCRIPT

After I had completed the rough draft of this chapter, I sent a copy of it to a cousin, Shirley Tubbs, who knew

Uncle Mickey quite well even though he was about a decade older than she. As a child, Shirley and her family often visited the Davises at the farm near Tuscola. On those visits, Shirley said, Uncle Mickey would give the children rides on the horse-drawn farm machinery and would entertain them in many other ways as well. He always took time from his busy schedule and had the necessary patience to make her and her brothers feel welcome and to show them an interesting and exciting time. Though nearly seventy years have elapsed since those visits, Shirley still remembers Uncle Mickey very fondly. Until he was declared missing in action, she and Mickey corresponded by letter, and they became even better acquainted.

Shirley's comments reminded me of the disturbing fact that Mickey died before he could have children of his own. How sad it is that, since his natural temperament seemed so well-suited for being a father, that he never had the opportunity to do so.

Irene (Thomas) Davis &
Melvin L. Davis
(1943)

American War Memorial
Colleville-sur-Mer, France

# CHAPTER 26

## IRENE, HARRY & THE TWO REDS

After Uncle Mickey's widow, Irene, signed off on the Davis farm and returned to her Virginia home, there was only sporadic contact between the two parts of the family. She did send an annual Christmas card and occasionally a short letter accompanied the card. In one of those letters Irene announced that she had married for a second time. We learned, too, that she and her new husband, who also was from Virginia, bought a home in suburban Richmond and continued to live there. From all reports the couple appeared to be very happy together and the marriage was a definite success.

Not until the early fall of 1956 did I have any further personal contact with Irene. In June of that year, after having taught high school in my home town of Vassar for only one year, I was inducted into the army. My initial eight weeks of basic infantry training were spent at Fort Leonard Wood, Missouri, and then I was transferred to Fort Lee, Virginia for advanced or specialized training at the Quartermaster Supply School there. Fort Lee, named for the Confederate commanding general, is located about thirty miles south of Richmond near the historic town of Petersburg, Virginia.

While in training at Fort Lee I had quite a lot of free time and in order to occupy myself, decided to see if I could locate the erstwhile Irene. After writing my mother for her new last name, I looked up Irene's number in the Greater Richmond Phone Book and made the call. She sounded very much the same (with the dulcet tones of her Southern Drawl still intact) and she seemed delighted to hear from me. We talked for a while and I filled her in on some of the Davis family members, all of whom she remembered well. In fact, she had more questions than we had time for, so she invited me to spend the following weekend with her and her husband, Harry.

All that week I wondered what sort of reception I would receive. After all, the last time I had seen Irene, I was a child in my early teens and she was an adult, married to my uncle. Would we find any common ground for conversation that could fill an entire weekend? And, how would Harry respond to me since I was a relative of Irene's first husband? I have to confess to being a bit apprehensive about the upcoming encounter.

Shortly after I arrived at Irene and Harry's home that weekend, I realized my worries had been unnecessary. Both of them welcomed me warmly like a prodigal son and they even had a delightful surprise waiting for me. Irene remembered that I had met her sister, Red, when they both had visited the Davis Clan in Michigan about ten years prior. The surprise was that Red and her husband were there as well. The five of us had a wonderful visit, though my enthusiasm was dampened somewhat when I learned the state of Irene's health. As near as I am able to figure, she was in her late thirties or early forties at the time. However, she had already experienced a life-threatening heart attack which left her seriously debilitated and in poor health. She was forced to retire early from her job and her physical condition required a severely restricted life style.

While we talked during that first evening's visit, I couldn't help but compare and contrast the two sisters, Irene and Red. Actually I wondered if they were, in fact, really blood sisters, but never had the temerity to broach the subject to them. Irene was an attractive, petite blonde with a tiny figure that was well proportioned and decidedly curvaceous. Red, however, was as large as Irene was small. She was tall, probably nearly six feet in height, and very broad. Red was not what I would call obese, instead she could legitimately be described by the old Yiddish term "zaftig," which means "full-bodied." Her enormous frame was topped off by a full head of shoulder-length, dark red curly hair.

Irene, like her husband, was the silent type. In addition, she was demure and somewhat shy. She spoke in a soft voice and rarely dominated any conversation. In direct contrast, Red was ever jolly, constantly breaking into loud and raucous laughter, thus showing one and all that she lived life on her own terms and enjoyed it to the fullest.

Where the sisters were alike was in their dealings with one another and the people with whom they came into contact. Irene and Red were extremely fond of each other and showed their sisterly love in hundreds of ways. They each had hearts as big as all outdoors and were generous to a fault. Both of them would go out of their way to keep from offending anyone. In addition, both Irene and Red accepted my army friends fully and always treated me as if I were a member of the family. Over the next couple of years I came to know them well and from those two ladies and their spouses, I learned the true meaning of the term "Southern Hospitality."

Red's husband also deserves a mention here because he too was such an interesting character. Impossible as it may seem, he was so big that he actually dwarfed his wife. Standing well over six feet in height, he had an enormous girth and a booming voice to match his physical dimensions. He was Red's equivalent in that he was as fun-loving and generous as she in all his dealings. His real name was Walter, but because of his enormous size and his carrot-red hair, he was nicknamed "Big Red." So, the result was, there were two Reds in the family instead of only one.

The two Reds lived in an apartment in downtown Richmond and drove a huge Buick Roadmaster automobile which, big as it was, never seemed quite able to contain them. To me they seemed larger than life itself. They were a fun-loving, childless couple whom I thoroughly enjoyed from the outset. After that first meeting at Irene's home, I spent nearly all of my weekend leaves from Fort Lee either in the company of the two Reds or with Irene and Harry. If I wanted a wild weekend, I visited the Reds, but if I wished to have a quieter time, then I chose the latter couple's home.

At the end of my training period at Fort Lee, I was transferred to Fort Jackson, South Carolina for the balance of my two year stint in the army. However, I continued to visit my "second family" in Virginia whenever the opportunity arose. We remained in relatively close contact until I was discharged from the army in 1958 and returned to teaching in Michigan. Eventually our correspondence began to dwindle and finally it ceased altogether. I <u>was</u> notified, however, when Irene suffered a second major heart attack and passed away as a result. Sadly, she hadn't yet reached the age of forty-five at the time. I am assuming that by now all of them have passed away. In the remote chance that they are still living today, Harry and the Two Reds would be in their early to mid nineties.

I much prefer to think of Big Red and "Little" Red as joyously tooling along in a gigantic Buick Roadmaster down a broad golden highway in the sky while Irene, Harry and even Uncle Mickey, smile serenely as they quietly observe the couple's antics from a sedate but lovely garden at the roadside.

# EPILOGUE

As I indicated in several of the chapters, one of my paramount interests in studying the genealogy of the family is to collect photographs of my direct ancestors. At the start I wasn't certain if pictures of those individuals even existed. What led me, you may ask, to start such a collection? Shortly after I retired from teaching in 1986, a distant cousin from Midland, Michigan sent my parents a picture of one of my great great grandfathers, Ebenezer Davis. The cousin, Caroline Ayre, did much family research in order to prove that she and her children and grandchildren were direct descendants of Ebenezer. His dubious fame lay in the fact that he and his family were the first permanent settlers of Tuscola County. Somewhere Caroline, while researching, located the old photo and, because she realized it was a family prize, had copies made and sent them to any members of the family she thought would be interested.

Mother and Dad showed me the photograph and I was amazed. There in front of me lay a picture of one of my ancestors who was born in the late 1700s, lived to the ripe old age of eighty-three and <u>died</u> over a hundred years ago. What an astounding find. The thought immediately popped into my head—if a photo of one of my great great grandparents existed, perhaps somewhere there might be pictures of my fifteen other great great grandparents. That was all it took to whet my appetite to learn if my theory were correct. I decided then to make the attempt to collect photographs of all of my direct antecedents.

Before I could begin searching for photographs of my ancestors, I had to learn just who they were. When one begins to add them up, family numbers increase dramatically. After all each person has two parents, four grandparents, eight great grandparents and sixteen great great grandparents. That makes a total of thirty. Then add to that number thirty-two great great great grandparents and it comes to a staggering sixty-two. Realistically a person of my age—I was about fifty-five at the time—could hope to find only a few photographs of his great great great grandparents because most were dead by the 1840s when photography became popular.

To start me in the right direction, Mother, with the help of her voluminous notes on the family, assisted me in making a diagram of my family tree. At that early date we were unable to fill in all the blanks, but at least it gave me a number of names for launching my quest.

How does one search for photographs of ancestors who have long since passed away? I'm not certain of the generally accepted method, but this was my plan of action. I wrote short letters to various people in all branches of the family—between thirty and forty altogether. In the letters I explained what I was attempting to do and asked if they knew of anyone in their part of the clan who possessed old photos. I also explained that if they would loan the pictures to me, I would have them copied and would return them in good condition. Or if they wished to have copies made I would be happy to reimburse their cost. Because of those requests a few photographs began to trickle in, so the tiny collection started to grow. Interestingly enough the search resulted in a number of new contacts with distant relatives who were previously unknown to me. Consequently, like my mother, through research I was increasing the numbers of my known relatives.

Another of my search methods involved attending all family reunions and get-togethers. Whenever possible I contacted the people doing the inviting and had them ask everyone ahead of time to bring their old photos to the meeting. That method, too, worked fairly well and over the next few years my pictorial family tree began to take shape. In 1997, when I had been collecting for about ten years, I moved from Michigan to New Mexico and by that date I had secured photographs of the following:

7 out of the 16 great great grandparents

7 out of the 8 great grandparents

4 out of the 4 grandparents

2 out of the 2 parents

Since then I have added three more great great grandparents' photos and now have 10 out of the 16 in that grouping. In addition to the above photos, I found one which is purported to be my great great great grandmother, Sarah (DeWitt) Rosencrants. The photo has never been authenticated so I don't usually include it with the others in the collection.

Since photographs are made for viewing, I had them matted and framed and then arranged in a group along one side of my bedroom. I call it my "Ancestral Wall." Each generation has its own row, starting from the top with the great great grandparents and leading in order down to my parents. Adding to the display, on the next row I hung photos of my three siblings and me. Below that I placed a picture of one of my older brother's sons and another of my sister's daughter. To complete the arrangement, the bottom row contains my brother's grandson and my sister's granddaughter. All in all there are seven generations of my family represented on the Ancestral Wall. As you can well imagine, the wall isn't large enough to include all of my sibling's children, grandchildren and great grandchildren so I opted to use only a representation of those generations.

I have chosen to end this book with a photograph of Ebenezer Davis and another of the Ancestral Wall. Ebenezer's photo provided me with the impetus to begin the collection and the Ancestral Wall was the end result. Thus they are the alpha and omega of the search.

It is my fervent hope that you have enjoyed this romp through the various generations of my family history. Many, many additional stories and photographs could have been included in the volume, but were omitted for one reason or another. I am certain that in every family there is an equal number of stories similar to the ones found here. It only takes someone willing to locate and then collect them into a book such as <u>Leafing Through My Family Tree</u>. I must confess that for me it was a labor of love.

Jerry R. Davis July,2007

Albuquerque, New Mexico

Ebenezer I. Davis
(1797 – 1880)

The Ancestral Wall

## ABOUT THE AUTHOR

Jerry R. Davis lived most of his life in Michigan's Lower Peninsula and earned bachelor's and master's degrees in history from universities there. He taught history and geography for 31 years in various junior high schools in Michigan before retiring in 1986. For the past ten years he has been an Albuquerque, New Mexico resident where he is a staff writer for <u>Posh New Mexico</u> magazine and a freelance writer for other venues. His previous non-fiction books were <u>Home on the Farm: Essays on a Michigan Childhood</u> (2003) and <u>Tales of the Road: Essays on a Half Century of Travel</u> (2004). He is a member of SouthWest Writers, an organization of New Mexico authors.